Writing About MOVIES

FIFTH EDITION

KAREN M. GOCSIK
University of California, San Diego

DAVE MONAHAN
University of North Carolina, Wilmington

RICHARD BARSAM
Emeritus, Hunter College

W. W. NORTON & COMPANY
New York • London

W. W. Norton & Company has been independent since its founding in 1923, when William Warder Norton and Mary D. Herter Norton first published lectures delivered at the People's Institute, the adult education division of New York City's Cooper Union. The firm soon expanded its program beyond the Institute, publishing books by celebrated academics from America and abroad. By midcentury, the two major pillars of Norton's publishing program—trade books and college texts—were firmly established. In the 1950s, the Norton family transferred control of the company to its employees, and today—with a staff of four hundred and a comparable number of trade, college, and professional titles published each year—W. W. Norton & Company stands as the largest and oldest publishing house owned wholly by its employees.

Printed in the United States of America.

Editor: Peter Simon
Senior project editor: Thomas Foley
Managing editor, College: Marian Johnson
Production manager: Elizabeth Marotta
Design director: Rubina Yeh
Series design: Chris Welch
Editorial assistant: Katie Pak
Composition: Westchester Publishing Services
Manufacturing: Sheridan Books, Inc.

ISBN: 978-0-393-66490-4

W. W. Norton & Company, Inc., 500 Fifth Avenue, New York, N.Y. 10110-0017
www.wwnorton.com
W. W. Norton & Company Ltd., Castle House, 75/76 Wells Street, London WIT 3QT

1 2 3 4 5 6 7 8 9 0

Writing About
MOVIES
FIFTH EDITION

Brief Contents

Part I: Preparing to Write

Part II: The Writing Process

Part III: Resources

Contents

Part I: Preparing to Write

Part II: The Writing Process

Part III: Resources

Writing About
MOVIES
FIFTH EDITION

Part I

PREPARING TO WRITE

1

The Challenges of Writing About Movies

What's so hard about writing about movies? After all, we all "know" movies. Most of us could recite the plot of *The Hunger Games* more easily than we could recite the Gettysburg Address. We know more about the fictional characters who inhabit "Middle Earth" in *The Lord of the Rings* trilogy than we know about many of the people who inhabit our own lives.

It's precisely our familiarity with film, however, that presents our greatest writing challenge. Film is so familiar and so prevalent in our lives that we are often lulled into viewing movies passively. As a result, certain aspects of films are often invisible to us. Caught up in the entertainment, we sometimes don't "see" the camera work, composition, editing, or lighting. Nor do we "hear" the sound design. Nor do we observe the production struggles that accompany every film—including the script's many rewrites, the drama of getting the project financed, the casting challenges, and the hundreds of other decisions that were strung together to make the film reach the screen.

However, when your film professor asks you to write about film, it's precisely those "invisible" aspects that you're expected to see and hear. You need to pay attention to the way the camera moves. Observe the composition (the light, shadow, and arrangement) within the frame. Think about how the film was edited. Note the sound design. In short, consider the elements that make up the film and examine how they function, separately and together. In breaking down the film into its constituent parts, you'll be able to *analyze* what you see.

You might also think about the film in the context of when it was made, how, and by whom. Considering the context of the film's production, its reception by viewing audiences, and its relationship with the culture in which it was made and released, you'll be able to *synthesize* your analysis of the film and its context. In short, you'll be able to write a paper that transforms your thoughts and responses into writing that is appropriately academic.

Before we get into the thick of this subject, let's tackle the most general question of all.

What Is Academic Writing?

Simply put, academic writing (sometimes called "scholarship") is writing done by scholars for other scholars—and that includes you. As a college student, you are engaged in activities that scholars have been engaged in for centuries: you read about, think about, argue about, and write about important, intriguing, or controversial ideas. Of course being a scholar requires that you read, think, argue, and write in certain ways. You will need to make and support your claims according to the customary expectations of the academic community.

How do you determine what these expectations are? The literary theorist Kenneth Burke has famously described scholarship as an ongoing conversation, and this metaphor may be helpful. Imagine you have just arrived at a dinner party. The discussion (which in this case is about cinema) has already been going on for quite a while when you arrive. What do you do? Do you sit down and immediately voice your opinions? Or do you listen, try to gauge the lay of the land, determine what contribution you might make, and only then venture to make it?

The etiquette that you would employ at the dinner party is precisely the strategy that you should use when you write academic papers. In short, listen to what other scholars are saying. Familiarize yourself with the scholarly conversation before jumping in. Pay attention to both *what* is said and *how* it is said. A book like the one you're reading now can be a helpful "dinner companion" that helps get you up to speed and fills you in on the conversation that preceded you. But you should make use of other resources, too. Your professor, for instance, is a living, breathing expert on what film scholars care about. Books, journals, and reputable Internet sites also offer an opportunity to eavesdrop on the ongoing scholarly conversation about movies. Once you understand the substance of that conversation, you can begin to construct informed arguments of your own.

Getting Started

CONSIDER WHAT YOU KNOW (AND WHAT YOU NEED TO KNOW)

A short paper written in response to a viewing of Alfred Hitchcock's *Rear Window* (1954), for example, may not require you to be familiar with Hitchcock's other films or to have a broad familiarity with film's formal elements. In other words, you don't need to "know" about a film—its history or how it's constructed—in order to formulate a response to it. All you need to know is what the film made you feel, or what it made you think about.

However, if you're asked to write an academic paper on the film, you'll need to know more. You'll need to have a firm grasp of the technical and formal elements of film so that you can explain how Hitchcock and his collaborators created the movie. You'll need to be familiar with Hitchcock's other films so that you can understand what themes are important to Hitchcock and his work. Finally, if you're watching this film in an upper-level film class, you'll need to be aware of different critical perspectives on Hitchcock's films and on films in general, so that you can "place" your argument within the ongoing critical conversation.

CONSIDER HOW TO THINK, ACADEMICALLY

The aim of thinking academically is to come up with new knowledge or new ideas. Scholars in all fields build on existing knowledge; they do not replicate what is known or what has already been said. Similarly, in terms of the film or films that you will write about, your goal is to come up with fresh observations. It's not enough to summarize in a paper what's obvious, or what's already known and discussed. You must also add something new, something of your own, to the ongoing scholarly conversation.

Understand, however, that "adding something of your own" is not an invitation to allow your personal associations, reactions, opinions, or experiences to dominate your paper. To create an informed argument, you must first recognize that your writing should be analytical rather than personal. In other words, your writing must show that your associations with, reactions to, and experiences of a film have been framed in a critical, rather than a personal, way.

This is not to say that your personal responses and opinions are irrelevant. Indeed, they are often good starting points for the academic work to come. For instance, being terrified by *The Babadook* (2014; director: Jennifer Kent) can be the first step on the way to a strong analysis. Interrogate your terror. Why are you scared? Which elements of the film contribute most to your fear? How does the film play with the horror genre in order to evoke a fear that is fresh and convincing?

Interrogating your personal responses is the first step in making sure that your argument will be appropriately academic. However, to further ensure that your responses are critical rather than personal, you will want to subject them to the following critical thinking processes: summary, evaluation, analysis, and synthesis.

SUMMARIZE

The first step in thinking critically about any film is to summarize what the film presents onscreen. You can construct several different summaries, depending on your goals, but beware: even the most basic of summaries—the plot summary—isn't as simple as it seems. It's difficult to write both economically and descriptively, to discern what's essential to your discussion and what's not.

Consider this: Orson Welles's *Citizen Kane* (1941) has a very complex plot using seven narrators and consisting of nine parts (five of which include flashback sequences). Further complicating matters is that the story duration is about seventy years, while the plot duration is one week of a reporter's research. *Citizen Kane* is a notoriously difficult film to sum up—though the following plot summary by Jesse Garon, taken from the Internet Movie Database (IMDb), does an excellent job:

> Multimillionaire newspaper tycoon Charles Foster Kane dies alone in his extravagant mansion, Xanadu, speaking a single word: "Rosebud." In an attempt to figure out the

> meaning of this word, a reporter tracks down the people who worked and lived with Kane; they tell their stories in a series of flashbacks that reveal much about Kane's life but not enough to unlock the riddle of his dying breath.

What makes this summary effective? It follows the basic structure of any film: a conflict/riddle/problem is proposed; someone tries to solve the problem, meeting obstacles along the way; finally, the problem is resolved. The writer of this summary traces the conflict without being sidetracked by the many plot complications. He sticks to the theme and to the basic conflict/resolution structure. He also makes sure that his sentences are simple and clear. In the end, he produces a summary that is faithful to the film but that doesn't overwhelm the reader with details.

The exercise of summarizing a film in this manner is a useful one. In most student film essays, plot summary is an important touchstone for the rest of the paper's argument: it helps to ground your argument in concrete details. Summarizing a film's plot helps you to see its structure, conflicts, and themes. But if you choose to provide a plot summary in your own writing, use it judiciously—as a tool that aids your analysis, not as an excuse to avoid analysis. A common beginner's error is to hand in a paper that claims to offer an argument about a film but instead merely retells the movie's story. You can avoid this by resisting the urge to structure your paper around the movie's narrative chronology. Use the narrative events to support your argument, but don't allow those events to overwhelm it.

When thinking critically about a film, you needn't limit yourself to plot summary. Equally useful, depending on your purpose, are summaries of a film's production values (lighting, editing, sound), its production history (financing, casting, distribution), or its critical reception (reviews, scholarship, and so on). The point is that summarizing is useful in helping you to clarify what you know about a film, laying the foundation for the more complex processes to come.

EVALUATE

Evaluation is an ongoing process. You can evaluate a film the moment you encounter it, and you can continue to evaluate and to reevaluate as you go along. It's important to understand that evaluating a movie is different from reacting to it. When you evaluate for an academic purpose, you must find and articulate the reasons for your personal response. What in the film is leading you to respond a certain way? Which influences that are not in the movie might be contributing to your response? Watching *Citizen Kane*, for instance, you might find yourself caught up in the film's suspense. What in the film is making you feel this way? The editing? The acting? The script? Something else? Can you point to a moment in the film that is particularly successful in creating suspense? In asking these questions, you are straddling two intellectual processes:

experiencing your own personal response, and analyzing the film.

Evaluation also encourages you to compare a film with other films that you've seen. How does the acting in *Citizen Kane* compare with the acting in other films from the same era? What about the editing? The composition and design of the images in the frame? The sound? The story? How do they compare? Evaluating what's special about a film allows you to isolate those aspects that are most interesting—and most fruitful—to investigate further.

ANALYZE

In the analysis stage of constructing an informed argument, your first task is to consider the parts of your topic that most interest you, and then examine how these parts relate to one another or to the whole. To analyze *Citizen Kane*, you will want to break the film down by examining particular scenes, point of view, camera movements, sound, and so on. In short, you'll want to ask, What are the components of Welles's film, and how do these components contribute to the film's theme? How do they contribute to Welles's work as a whole?

Films are filled with so much information that it is difficult to see even a small part of their formal and narrative arrangement in one viewing. You can learn a good deal by carefully analyzing individual shots and scenes, viewing them several times, and taking notes each time. Multiple viewings enable you to recognize how the parts of a film interrelate, how some elements recall previous events and foreshadow others, how motifs and subplots function, and how actors create characters through voice, gesture, and expression. When analyzing complex scenes, you might focus on one particular formal or narrative element in each viewing: lighting, editing, camera movement, setting, costume, dialogue, music, sound effects, and so forth.

When you analyze, you break the whole into parts so that you might see the whole differently. When you analyze, you find things to say.

SYNTHESIZE

When you synthesize, you look for *connections* between ideas. Consider once again *Citizen Kane*. In analyzing this film, you might come up with elements that seem initially disparate. You might have some observations that at first don't seem to jell. Or you might have read various critical perspectives on the film, all of them in disagreement with one another. Now would be the time to consider whether these disparate elements or observations might be reconciled, or synthesized. This intellectual exercise requires that you create an *umbrella argument*—a larger argument under which several observations and perspectives might stand.

In an analysis of *Citizen Kane*, for example, you might observe a series of elements that initially seem at odds with one another. For instance, you might note the range of conflicting emotions that the actors experience (each shifts among various feelings that include tenderness, joy, annoyance, guilt, and rage), and how the interior and exterior actions contradict our typical expectations (whereas outside in the snow the boy Charles plays gleefully, inside the house, which one would expect to be warmer, the lamps remain unlit and the action is cold and strained). You might argue that, by calling our attention to these conflicting aspects of the film, Welles is constructing a scene in which appearances are deceiving. Through this scene, you get the sense that any interpretation of the film's surface details might be mistaken. This warning leads you to think more broadly about what Welles might be saying—about appearances, and about the secrets that we hold within. You might then be inspired to look for other examples in which Welles seems to be commenting on appearances, and synthesize them into a broader observation of the film. In this way, you will be able to transform a list of observations into a powerful and intriguing argument.

Adopting a Rhetorical Stance

When writing an academic paper, you must consider not only what you want to say but also the audience to whom you're saying it. In other words, it's important to determine not only what you think about a topic but also what your audience is likely to think. What biases does your audience have? What values, expectations, and knowledge do they possess? For whom are you writing, and for what purpose?

When you begin to answer these questions, you have started to reckon with what has been called the "rhetorical stance," which refers to the position you take as a writer in terms of both the subject and the reader of your paper.

CONSIDER YOUR POSITION

Let's first consider your relationship to the topic you're writing about. The first thing that you'll want to determine when approaching your topic is what kind of paper you are being asked to compose. In other words, the assignment will let you know what kind of relationship you are expected to develop with your topic. For example, if you are asked to write an argument paper, you are being encouraged to take a stand. Maybe you've been asked to write a paper about the film industry's habit of hiring "abled" actors to play disabled characters. Do you support this practice? Do you challenge it? Do you support it for some reasons, but challenge it for others? Regardless of what position you take, you need to have a clear sense of your "relationship" to that topic so that you can communicate clearly to your reader where you stand, and why.

More often in your film class you will be asked to write not an argument paper but an analysis paper—a paper that looks at *how* something is constructed and then offers an argument regarding the effectiveness or the implications of that construction. (We discuss at length the process of writing an analytical paper in "Analyzing Film," later in this guide.) For now, it's sufficient to note that writing an analysis paper also requires you to *make an argument*. In other words, when you analyze a film, you don't want simply to describe what the director, or editor, or costume designer did. You also want to indicate why these decisions matter—why these decisions were important to the film, or to filmmaking in general. You'll also want to convey to your reader a sense of why your analysis matters to the ongoing conversation about the film. In the end, argument is a crucial part of any analysis paper.

To ensure that your relationship to your topic is appropriately analytical or argumentative, ask yourself some questions. First, consider whether your relationship to your topic is rooted in argument and analysis, or in opinion. What's the difference? Opinion is subjective and can be justified by the opinion holder's personal tastes and preferences; analysis and argument require more objective evidence and must be defended via reason. To ensure that you are producing argument or analysis rather than opinion, you will first want to consider why you chose this particular topic. Why did you find this film, or some aspect of it, more important or interesting than others? What personal feelings or biases does the film (or this aspect of the film) engage? Can you defend this bias critically? Have you thought carefully about responses to the film that might challenge yours? Might some part of your response to the movie cause readers to discount your paper as one-sided or uncritical? If any of these questions raise a flag for you, rethink your relationship with your topic with these questions in mind. Use them to transform personal opinion into academic analysis/argument.

CONSIDER YOUR AUDIENCE

Your position on a topic does not, by itself, determine your rhetorical stance. You must also consider your readers. In the college classroom, the audience is usually your professor and your classmates—although occasionally your professor will instruct you to write for a more particular or more general audience. No matter who your readers are, you'll want to consider them carefully before you start to write.

What do you know about your readers and their stance toward your topic? What are they likely to know about the topic? What biases are they likely to have? Moreover, what effect do you hope to have on the readers? Is your aim to be controversial? Informative? Entertaining? Will the readers appreciate or resent your intention?

Once you've determined who your readers are, you will want to consider how you might best reach them. If, for example, you're an authority on a particular subject and you're writing to readers who know little or nothing about that subject, you'll want to take an informative stance. If you aren't yet confident about a topic and you have more questions than answers, you might want to take an inquisitive stance.

In any case, when you're deciding on a rhetorical stance, choose one that allows you to be sincere. You don't want to take an authoritative stance on a subject if you cannot be confident about what you're saying. On the other hand, don't avoid taking a position on a subject; readers are very often frustrated by writers who refuse to take a clear stance. What if you are of two minds on a subject? Declare that to the reader. Make ambivalence your clear rhetorical stance.

Finally, don't write simply to please your professor. Though some professors find it flattering to discover that all of their students share their positions on a subject, most of us are hoping that your argument will engage us by telling us something new about your topic—even if that "something new" is simply a fresh emphasis on a minor detail. Moreover, it's impossible for you to replicate the ideal paper that exists in your professor's head. When you try, you risk having your analysis compared to your professor's. Is that really what you want?

Considering Tone and Style

So now you understand what's required of you in an academic paper. You need to be analytical. You need to create an informed argument. You need to consider your relationship to the topic and to the reader. But there is one more aspect of your writing that you must consider—particularly in terms of your relationship with your reader—and that is the tone and style of your work.

The tone and style of academic writing might at first seem intimidating. Students new to academic writing sometimes feel that they have to employ the jargon and complex sentences that they find in scholarship. But that's not the case. Professors don't want imitation scholarship. They want students to write clearly and intelligently on matters that they, the students, care about. The tone of an academic paper must be clear and inviting. Your task is to render a good idea in clear language that is a pleasure to read.

After all, professors are human beings, capable of boredom, laughter, irritation, and awe. They have lives outside of their duties as teachers, and they don't appreciate having their time wasted any more than you do. Understand that you're writing to a person who will be delighted when you make your point clearly, concisely, and persuasively. Understand, too, that they will be less delighted if you have inflated your prose, pumped up your page count, or tried to impress them by using terms that you didn't take the time to understand. (For more on how to craft an appropriate but engaging academic tone and style, see "Attending to Style," later in this guide.)

2

Looking at Movies

Before you start writing anything about a movie, you must first look at it—closely, with an analytical eye, and armed with the specialized vocabulary that is an integral part of serious film study. Looking closely at movies, and taking notes as you do so, is the first step toward having something interesting to say about them. This chapter should help you to get the process started.

Public and Private Screenings

Most film courses require attendance at public screenings. Often the movies being viewed are the ones that your professor wants you to write about. Even if public screenings aren't required by your instructor, viewing a movie with an audience in a theater is something that every student of film should experience. The reaction of your fellow audience members may, after all, be different from yours. Being alert to their reactions could help you to notice things about the film that you might have overlooked if your only screening happened in the privacy of your own room. Use the time in a public screening to enjoy the experience along with the audience, but also to note those moments when the audience reacts strongly to what's happening onscreen. If you can manage it, take shorthand notes (as discreetly as possible) about what was happening onscreen immediately before, during, and after those moments. These notes will be valuable when you later view the movie in private.

There was a time not so long ago when scholars, critics, and students of film were forced to write about movies without the benefit of private viewings after public screenings. Relying on notes and memory, they often got the details wrong, sometimes in ways that undercut the arguments they were attempting to make. Thankfully, those days are past. Most of the movies that instructors assign in film courses are also available in digital formats for private viewing. These formats have been tremendously popular with consumers, obviously, but they are also a godsend for film scholars and film students, who can rewind, fast-forward, pause, and select specific scenes as often as they need to.

The benefits of private viewings and these simple playback options for film analysis can't be overstated. The pause button, for example, allows you to look carefully at the composition of a shot, to note details of the setting, design, lighting, and individual characters' appearance. The ability to watch a scene first with the sound on, then with the sound off, and then to close your eyes and listen only to the sound in that scene, can help you to isolate the effects of the visual and auditory elements individually, and thus understand how that scene "works" with more precision. Even fast-forwarding through a film that you've already viewed can reveal things about the movie: for instance, the repetition of certain patterns, motifs, or visual themes that might not have been obvious when viewed at regular speed.

Not only do digital formats allow you to view movies in a more accurate and productive way, but they also frequently give you access to contextual information about the film that might be difficult to find otherwise. Many DVDs, for example, provide special features that document the film's production background, the intentions and plans of its creators, and the technological innovations and techniques that made certain things happen onscreen. They also often include scenes and shots that were cut from the film. Viewing unused footage provides further insight into the decision-making process of the filmmakers. Sometimes, a scene is cut because of a poor acting performance, or an entire subplot is removed because it doesn't seem to work. Other times, very good scenes and strong performances are left on the cutting room floor. The decision to remove such scenes sometimes reflects the desires of a director to tell the story more concisely or simply, and other times is a signal that a producer or other executive has pushed for a shorter running time. Since many deleted scenes were dropped before they underwent sound editing, effects work, and color corrections (that is, they are *rough cuts*), this unused footage also provides dramatic evidence of the degree to which film studios polish the final product—a useful reminder that the supposed "realism" of the final release is always a carefully crafted construction.

Coupled with the wealth of information on the Internet, special DVD features provide film students with an abundance of material once reserved only for industry insiders or researchers lucky enough to be granted access to studios, film libraries, and special collections. You should take advantage of this material as much as is relevant to your writing assignment.

The Importance of Taking Notes

Taking notes is an essential part of preparing to write about movies. Whether you are recording your observations during a public or personal screening, copying key points of a classroom lecture or group discussion, or jotting down stray ideas over the course of your day, note taking can capture observations, attitudes, and insights that you may otherwise not recall when the time comes to actually compose your paper. Memory is less perfect than we often assume, and realizing that "memory," especially in academic settings, exists no less in documents than between our ears should encourage you to adopt good note-taking practices. There are no rules for note taking, but here are a few useful hints to start:

Make your notes as succinct as possible.

Resist the temptation to record all of your observations at once. Focus instead on significant turning points and details. You can always return to the film for more detail later.

Make rough sketches of shots that you want to discuss. These will prove very useful when you begin to write. If you're viewing on a computer, you can also use an inexpensive software program to grab images from the movie and insert them into your paper as illustrations.

Use shorthand for describing what you see onscreen (a list of suggested shorthand notations is provided at the end of the book). This shorthand will not only speed up the process but will get you in the habit of using film terms.

If you're viewing the movie on a player of some sort, make note of the timing of each shot that you want to discuss—for instance, 09:43—so that you can easily find it again if you need to. If you're watching in a theater, note the approximate timing (e.g., "approx. 10:00").

Review and organize your notes according to any patterns or categories that may appear. Do this while the viewing is still fresh in your mind. Many students come up with ideas for their papers when they reorganize the observations in their notes.

Taking notes is a highly personal activity. Some people meticulously record information in a systematic way, while others haphazardly scrawl ideas and doodles. You should adopt whatever method works for you. That said, there are a few strategies for note taking that have proven useful to film scholars and students that you might consider using or adapting to your own purposes:

ASKING WHY

When viewing a film for the first time all the way through, the main priority is to be alert to things about the film that strike you as different, memorable, or puzzling at the moment of viewing. Taking note of these things, and framing your notes about them in the form of questions, will prompt you during your viewing(s) to return to those moments to see if you can answer that question, and thus perhaps discover something about the movie that is interesting enough to write about. Here are some concrete examples of questions about specific films that a student might ask:

Why is every shot linked to a single character as a close-up, over-the-shoulder shot, or point-of-view shot [in Darren Aronofsky's *Mother!*]?

Why do the credits run at the beginning [of Stanley Kubrick's *Spartacus*] rather than at the end?

Why is the last shot [in François Truffaut's *The 400 Blows*] a freeze-frame?

Why is the first running sequence [in Tom Tykwer's *Run Lola Run*] partly done in animated cartoon form?

Why does the camera "look away" at the moment when Vic Vega cuts off Marvin Nash's ear [in Quentin Tarantino's *Reservoir Dogs*]?

Why is the dialogue so hard to hear [in Christopher Nolan's *Dunkirk*]?

Why are there two actresses playing the same role in the same scene [in Luis Buñuel's *That Obscure Object of Desire*]?

Questions such as these will plant the seeds for productive re-viewing, analysis, and writing.

PLOT SEGMENTATION

If you suspect, after your first question-generating note-taking session, that you will need to understand the structure of the movie's narrative system in order to write your paper, then you may want to create a *plot segmentation*—a scene-by-scene outline of the entire film—during your first re-viewing. In a plot segmentation, each scene should be described briefly in a separate line, with whatever plot details strike you as worth noting (for example, events that inform or relate to character or story development later in the film.) How will you know when you've gone from one scene to another? When a film significantly shifts in time or space, a new scene has begun. You will soon discover that even seemingly straightforward narratives are often in fact complex chains of cause and effect. A plot summary will greatly aid your understanding of a movie's narrative system, but it will probably require a significant investment of your time and attention. Here's a plot segmentation of the first ten minutes of John Ford's *Stagecoach* (1939):

1. A cavalry horseman and Native American scout ride into Tonto.

2. The horseman and scout report that Apache chief Geronimo is on the warpath. A telegraph operator gets the message "Geronimo" just before the telegraph lines go dead.

3. The stagecoach arrives in Tonto and delivers a payroll strongbox. Lucy Mallory, a passenger, is observed by the "notorious gambler" Hatfield. We learn that she has traveled from the east to reunite with her cavalry officer husband.

4. Buck, the stagecoach driver, visits Marshal Curley Wilcox, from whom he learns that the Ringo Kid has escaped from prison and is rumored to be seeking revenge on Luke Plummer, the man who killed his father and brother. When Buck reveals that he recently saw Plummer in Lordsburg, the sheriff announces that he will travel with the stagecoach to Lordsburg.

5. The payroll strongbox is delivered to Gatewood, the Tonto banker.

6. Dallas (a prostitute) and Doc Boone are ordered to leave Tonto (via the stagecoach) by the Tonto Ladies Law and Order League.

7. Doc visits the saloon where we learn he has been more than a regular customer. He meets and immediately attaches himself to a fellow stagecoach passenger: the mild-mannered Peacock, a traveling whiskey salesman.

8. A fresh team of horses is harnessed to the stagecoach.

9. Gatewood removes the payroll from the safe and slips it into a valise.

This brief excerpt demonstrates how the plot of *Stagecoach* establishes a number of elements central to our understanding and appreciation of film's narrative.

- The central goal: Survive the stagecoach trip to Lordsburg.
- The antagonist opposing the pursuit of that goal: Geronimo and his warriors.
- Setting: A wild frontier rife with vigilante justice, murder, and renegade warriors.
- Essential character and plot information regarding eight of the nine protagonists, including their relationship to the central goal.
- The protagonist, goal, and antagonists of an important secondary plot: Ringo's quest for revenge, which is opposed by both his fellow protagonist Marshal Curley Wilcox and the outlaw Luke Plummer.

SHOT-ANALYSIS CHARTS

Sometimes, your instructor will tell you to pay special attention to a particular scene in the movie you're writing about. Or, if the topic of your paper is yours to determine, you may realize after a few viewings that a particular scene in a movie may be critically important to your paper. Either way, a useful note-taking strategy when you want to analyze a specific scene is the *shot-analysis chart*. A shot-analysis chart, like the plot segmentation, is a "map" of sorts that allows you to see the shot-by-shot structure of a scene, and thus to understand better how the scene works.

The simplest version of a shot-analysis chart would offer four columns and as many rows as there are discrete shots. The columns would be as shown in the sample chart that follows of the beginning of a scene in *Stagecoach* that emphasizes the social division between the ensemble of protagonists: one column for numbering each shot, one that describes each shot in enough detail for you to be able to recall its details when you later write about it, one that specifies the duration of the shot, and finally, one that specifies the type of shot (using a shorthand notation). While the shot-analysis chart might initially seem too technical and detailed for your work as a novice film analyst, you'll find that taking the time to create this chart will actually save you time when you start putting together your analysis—you won't have to keep returning to the film to note the shot sequence, duration, and so on.

Shot number	*Description*	*Length (sec.)*	*Type of shot*
1	The passengers (minus Ringo and Dallas) gather for a meal.	9	LS
2	Ringo invites Dallas to sit at the table.	3	MFS
3	Gatewood, Hatfield, and Lucy react with distaste.	3	MFS
4	Lucy hesitates, then sits. Ringo sits beside her. Camera tracks in.	13	MFS to MS
5	Lucy stares offscreen (toward Dallas).	3	MCU
6	Dallas returns the look (offscreen toward Lucy), and then lowers eyes.	7	MCU
7	Hatfield places plate before Lucy, and looks (offscreen) toward Dallas.	10	MFS
8	Ringo places plate before Dallas, and looks (offscreen) toward Hatfield.	3	M2S
9	Hatfield offers to find Lucy another place at the table.	6	MFS
10	Ringo looks (offscreen) toward Hatfield.	2	M2S
11	Lucy accepts Hatfield's offer, rises, and walks to other end of table.	8	MFS
12	Hatfield seats Lucy at far end of table. Gatewood moves to join her.	17	LS
13	Blaming himself, Ringo rises to leave. Lucy stops him. Ringo serves her food.	24	M2S

LS = Long Shot
MFS = Medium Full Shot
MS = Medium Shot
MCU = Medium Close-Up
M2S = Medium Two Shot

You might choose to get into more detail by adding other columns. To chart a particularly kinetic scene, for example, you might want to describe the movement of the camera and the movement of figures within the frame. If you suspect that the setting of each shot in a scene is somehow crucial to the argument that you'll want to make, then you probably should add a column specifically dedicated to a description of the setting. If the sound in the film seems to be playing a crucial role in the scenes you're analyzing, then you will want to add a column that allows you to specify the types and sources of sound in each shot. Whether spare or detailed, the main purpose of a shot-analysis chart is to accurately map the progress from one shot to another in the scene. This sort of note taking will help you to be precise in your descriptive analysis when you finally write your paper.

What Are You Looking For?

You may wonder at this point just what all these tools and tips amount to. What, exactly, are you *looking for*? What's the *point*?

To answer these questions, first we need to recognize that every movie is a complex synthesis—a combination of many separate, interrelated elements that form a coherent whole. Anyone attempting to comprehend a complex synthesis must rely on analysis—the act of taking something complicated apart to figure out what it is made of and how it all fits together.

A chemist, for example, breaks down a compound substance into its constituent parts to learn more than just a list of ingredients. The goal usually extends to determining how the identified individual components work together toward some sort of outcome: What is it about this particular mixture that makes it taste like strawberries, or grow hair, or kill cockroaches? Likewise, film analysis involves more than breaking down a sequence, a scene, or an entire movie to identify the tools and techniques that are used to create it. The investigation is also concerned with the function and potential effect of that combination: Why does it make you laugh, or prompt you to tell your friend to see it, or incite you to join the Peace Corps? The search for answers to these sorts of questions boils down to one essential inquiry: What does it mean?

Intriguingly, movies have a way of hiding their methods and meanings. When movies are consumed the way they were designed to be consumed (i.e., as entertainment, in one uninterrupted sitting), then their methods, and even their underlying meanings, fade into the background—they become "invisible" to the viewer.

The moving aspect of moving pictures is one reason for this invisibility. Movies simply move too fast for even the most diligent viewer to consider everything they've seen. When we read a book, we can pause to ponder the meaning of any word, sentence, or passage. Our eyes often flit back to review something we've already read. Similarly, we can stand and study a painting or sculpture for as long as we require in order to absorb whatever meaning we need or want from it. But up until very recently, our relationship with movies has been transitory. We experience movie shots—each of which is capable of delivering multiple layers of visual and auditory information—for the briefest of moments before they are taken away and replaced with another, and another, and another. If you're watching a movie the way it's designed to be experienced, you're absorbed in what you're seeing. There's no time (and perhaps no desire) to contemplate the layers of meanings that a single movie moment might present.

Recognizing a spectator's tendency to identify with the camera's viewpoint (which may be omniscient or that of an individual or group), early filmmakers created a film grammar (or cinematic language) that draws upon the way we interpret visual or audio information in our real lives, thus allowing audiences to absorb movie meaning intuitively and instantly. Cinematic language is a verbal and nonverbal method of communication that uses formal elements to express a movie's thoughts and feelings. These elements are narrative, mise-en-scène (the staging and composition of elements in the frame), cinematography, acting, editing, and sound.

In the hands of film artists, the flexibility of this language is what makes movies some of the most visceral experiences that art has to offer. For example, the more you learn about the properties of the movie camera, the more you will understand how rich its potential is, not only to record, but also to manipulate the world we see on the screen. And this is why we say that everything you see (or hear) has been put there for a reason, whether it's the way an actor performs, the way an editor creates rhythm in a sequence, or the way sound technicians enhance emotion with tone or volume. The film artist commands cinematic language with a power equal to that of an author writing a novel. Indeed, it is a greater power, for the director works with many artistic and technical collaborators, while the author ordinarily works alone.

So, what are you looking for? In short, you are looking for specific examples of cinematic language that will support the principal idea of your paper. Let's say that you have chosen to write about how Spike Lee develops the theme of power in *Do the Right Thing* (1989), a classic film about racial and ethnic tensions in a New York City neighborhood. Lee made a film rather than a novel because sight and sound seemed to him to be the most realistic ways to capture the vigorous movement and energy of a large city and colorful cast of characters. He tells his story using cinematic language (or film grammar), meaning that instead of telling us, as a novelist does, he shows us with such expressive elements as cinematography, acting, editing, and sound that create not only shots, but also meaning.

Let's say that, from your classroom discussions and background preparation, you have reached two hypotheses: that each of Lee's characters have their own ideas about power, and that their individual ideas play out in larger conflicts between a range of opposing forces of race, ethnicity, family, gender, culture, and philosophy. So, in your first analytical screening, you will be looking for examples of how ideas of power are expressed in cinematography, editing, or sound. As you watch the film, you find that the camera is almost always moving as it records the characters' continuous activity, the editing maintains that pace, and the sound (which is realistic and diegetic, often from a boom box) is loud and vibrant. There is *power* in this movement and volume.

This is just a start. Although these examples demonstrate the interdependent relationship of cinematic form and content, *Do the Right Thing* is not a film that should be evaluated strictly on just formal standards. Its meanings are also a product of social contexts bigger than what's on the screen. Remember that your examples must not only support your position but also consider your readers—what sort of context would they bring to a reading of *Do the Right Thing*?

Armed with some tips and techniques to analyze the formal elements that make up a movie's cinematic language, you will be better able to appreciate the complex way in which they blend to convey meaning. There's no way of knowing what your instructor will require in a writing assignment, but the chances are that it will involve analyzing the interaction of form and content—for example, how editing helps to create meaning in Alfred Hitchcock's *The Birds* (1963).

3

Formal Analysis

In the previous chapter, we focused on the elements of movies that are there on the screen for us to see. Analyzing those elements—a process sometimes referred to as *formal analysis*—is an important part (in many cases even the *dominant* part) of the process of writing about movies. But it isn't the only approach you'll want to consider. In this chapter, we will briefly describe the various analytical approaches—starting with formal analysis—that serious students of film are asked to employ in their writing.

What Is Formal Analysis?

Careful analysis of a film's form is an essential skill for any student of cinema. Nearly all essays about movies will employ formal analysis, even ones that are written primarily from another perspective.

So what is formal analysis? Formal analysis dissects the complex synthesis of cinematography, sound, composition, design, movement, performance, and editing as they are orchestrated by screenwriters, directors, cinematographers, actors, editors, sound designers, and art directors, as well as the many craftspeople who implement their vision. This synthesis seems complex because it is: the meaning of a movie is expressed through the complicated interplay of its many formal elements. These elements range from matters as straightforward as where and when a particular scene takes place, to the subtler issues of mood, tone, and what a character is thinking or feeling.

While it is certainly possible for the overeager analyst to read more meaning into a particular visual or audio component than the filmmaker intended, you should consider that cinematic storytellers exploit every tool at their disposal. Every element in every frame exists for a reason. Your task, as a formal analyst, is to carefully consider the narrative intent of each of these elements. You'll want to consider how the parts of a film interrelate, how some elements recall previous events and foreshadow others, how motifs and subplots function, how actors create characters through voice, gesture, and expression, and how directors, cinematographers, sound technicians, and editors create mood and convey meaning.

When analyzing complex scenes, you might focus on one particular element: lighting or editing, camera movement or costume, music or sound effects, and so forth. While not all scenes will reward such close attention, most films contain segments that are layered with meaning and significance. If you take the time to examine the way that form and content work together to create meaning, you'll certainly find interesting ideas that can serve as the foundation for your paper.

DESCRIBING FILM FORM

Whatever formal element or elements you choose to write about, you need to offer your reader dynamic, detailed, descriptive writing. In other words, you need to *show*, not merely *tell*, your readers what happens. While your essays cannot provide your reader with images twenty feet tall or offer up enhanced surround sound, they can evoke—through language—something of the film's form and your experience of it. Also important to note is that a good description can be analytical: the way you *describe* a scene or shot can convey your *analysis* of that scene or shot. For these reasons it's important to craft your descriptions with great care.

Let's look at a few descriptions of the opening sequence of Alfred Hitchcock's *Vertigo* (1958). In the first example, notice that although the writer has something to say, the writing offers very little detailed imagery:

> The theme of vertigo can be seen even in the opening credits. The close-up of a woman's face and the music make one think of psychological problems. The circles that begin to appear seem like a vertigo of some kind. The opening makes it clear that the movie *Vertigo* will be about more than just the fear of heights.

This writing doesn't offer a vivid description of the opening of the film. We don't get a sense of what the woman's face looks like. Nor do we know what sort of music might be playing that would make us understand that we are looking at a woman who is unstable. Moreover, this description doesn't connect the descriptive details to the analysis: the writer *tells* us what we should be thinking, but doesn't *show* us why we should be thinking that way. In sum, the writer has squandered an opportunity to write a description that also shapes her analysis.

The next example, by the film critic and scholar Robin Wood, is more descriptive. Note that Wood not only practices the principle of *Show, don't tell*; he also shapes his description in order to make his analytical points:

> One aspect of the theme of *Vertigo* is given to us by Saul Bass's credit designs. We see a woman's face; the camera moves in first to lips, then to eyes. The face is blank, mask-like, representing the inscrutability of appearances: the impossibility of knowing what goes on behind the mask. But the eyes dart nervously from side to side: beneath the mask are imprisoned unknown emotions, fears, desperation. Then a vertiginous, spiraling movement begins in the depths of the eye, moving outward as if to involve the spectator. Before the film has begun, we are made aware that the vertigo of the title is to be more than a literal fear of heights.[1]

[1] Robin Wood, *Hitchcock's Films Revisited* (New York: Columbia University Press, 1989), p. 110.

Wood's analysis of the opening credit sequence works both because he helps us to *see* the opening sequence, and because he illustrates the theme of vertigo—an abstraction—via his concrete description of what is projected onscreen.

Whatever formal element or elements you focus on when you analyze a film, make sure that you use language that is as vivid and descriptive as possible. Tie the concrete details and the carefully constructed observations to larger themes and ideas as you see fit, but always make sure that the particulars within the film back you up. Getting the details right is the heart and soul of formal analysis.

DOING FORMAL ANALYSIS: A SCREENING CHECKLIST

As you examine a movie's formal elements, keep in mind the following questions and considerations. For your convenience, we've crafted this list according to the primary categories of film form: narrative, mise-en-scène, cinematography, acting, editing, and sound. If you are uncertain about the meaning of any of the terms used in the following pages, you should consult the "Illustrated Glossary of Film Terms" at the end of this book. If you're eager for more complete discussions of these terms, you should consult a more comprehensive text, such as *Looking at Movies: An Introduction to Film*.

In general

Whenever you prepare a formal analysis of a scene's use of film grammar, start by considering the filmmakers' intent. Remember that filmmakers use every cinematic tool at their disposal. Very little in any movie moment is left to chance. So before analyzing any scene, first ask yourself some basic questions:

What is this scene about?
After watching this scene, what do I understand about the character's thoughts and emotions?
How did the scene make me feel?
What tools and techniques did the filmmakers use in order to communicate these feelings?
Are there elements of the film that I might not have picked up on in the first viewing?
Did I have any expectations of the movie before I watched it? What were these expectations? Where did they come from? How did they shape my reaction to the movie?
What can I learn from the movie's title? What did the title suggest to me before I saw the movie? What does it suggest now that I've seen it? Has my understanding of the title (or the movie) changed?

Narrative

Narrative is not only the story being told on the screen, but also the cinematic and other devices that help tell that story.

Analyzing narrative means examining the effect of a narrator, the relationships of characters, heroes pursuing goals and villains thwarting their progress; it means taking stock of individual scenes and how they fit into the overall plot, and the sequence in which plot points are arranged in cause-and-effect relationships. Questions that can help you to examine narrative elements closely include the following:

Do I see any narrative or visual patterns recurring? If so, what are these patterns, and why is the director repeating them?

Who is the movie's protagonist? What motivates or complicates that character's actions?

What might I learn from categorizing the movie's characters according to their depth (round characters versus flat characters) and motivation?

Is the camera the only narrator of the film (in other words, is the camera the vehicle by which viewers are "told" the story of the movie)? Or is there another narrator, provided to the viewer by voice-over or direct address?

Does the movie use restricted narration to limit the viewer's perspective? If so, what is the effect on the viewer's understanding?

What is the movie's narrative structure? What is the inciting incident? What goal does the protagonist pursue? What obstacles does the protagonist encounter, and how does she handle them? How is the problem resolved?

Are the plot events presented in chronological order? If not, how are events ordered? Why were they ordered this way?

What can I learn from the movie's subplot? What does this subplot add to the movie? Why is it there?

What nondiegetic elements (e.g., voice-overs) are essential to the movie's plot? Do they seem natural and appropriate to the film, or do they appear to be "tacked on" to make up for a shortcoming in the narrative?

Are there scenes that create a noticeable summary relationship between story duration and screen duration? How do these scenes complement or detract from the overall narrative?

Is any major plot event presented onscreen more than once? If so, why do you think the filmmaker has chosen to repeat the event?

Mise-en-scène

Mise-en-scène ("staging or putting on an action or scene" in French) refers to the staging of everything we see in every shot. Aspects of mise-en-scène include the design of sets, costumes, makeup, and props, as well as the composition of shots (i.e., how characters and objects are framed, and their organization, balance, distribution, and movement within that frame). The interplay of design and composition, and the relative emphasis of some elements of both, help create meaning in each shot and scene. The following questions can help you deduce which elements of the mise-en-scène help create this overall feel and thus your response to a movie:

How am I responding emotionally to the movie's design and mise-en-scène? Am I comforted or made anxious by what I see onscreen?

What elements contribute to my emotional response?

Does the movie's design feel coherent to me? Do the various elements of the design (the sets, props, costumes, makeup, hairstyles, etc.) work together, or do some elements work against others? What is the effect either way?

Do the design and mise-en-scène evoke the correct times, spaces, and moods? Or is there something "not quite right" that distracts me?

Does it seem as though the filmmakers were attempting to achieve a "realistic" look with the design and mise-en-scène of this film? If so, have the filmmakers succeeded in that goal?

If making the mise-en-scène seem "realistic" doesn't appear to be important in this movie, what were the filmmakers attempting to accomplish with their design?

How are the individual shots framed? What is the composition within the frame? Where are the figures placed? What is the relationship among the figures in the foreground, middle ground, and background?

Does the film employ an open frame or a closed frame? What visual clues suggest that the framing is open or closed? What is the effect of this framing on the viewer's understanding?

Does the use of light call attention to itself? What effect does the lighting have on the overall meaning of the scene? On the overall meaning of the movie?

Does the shot or scene employ lots of movement? Very little movement? How does this movement complement or detract from the narrative?

Cinematography

Broadly speaking, cinematography is the process of capturing moving images on film. Movies have their own language, and cinematography could be called film's grammar—how that language works to make meaning. Cinematography consists of a filmmaker's choices about the types of shots, quality of lighting, camera angles, and special effects to create the language of cinema, in much the same way as a writer picks her nouns, verbs, and adjectives to create meaning on a page. And just as specific words have different connotations, different choices in the cinematography of a film create different meanings and associations on the screen. When analyzing a film's cinematography, consider some of the following questions:

Is the film shot so that I identify with the camera lens? If so, what does the director compel me to see? What is left to my imagination? In sum, how does the director's use of the camera help to create the movie's meaning?

Do the cinematographic aspects of the film—the qualities of the film stock, lighting, lenses, framing, camera angles, camera movement, and use of long takes—add up to an overall look? How can I describe that look?

Which moments in the film convey information that is not reflected in characters' action and dialogue? How do these scenes convey that information?

Are special effects used in the film? To what extent? Are they appropriate to and effective in telling the story? Are they effective in making something look real when it isn't?

What kinds of shots am I noticing? Is the cinematographer employing shots other than the medium shot—for instance, extreme close-ups or extreme long shots? What role are these shots playing in the film?

Is the cinematographer deviating from eye-level shots? If there are high-angle shots or low-angle shots, are these shots meant to represent a particular point of view (i.e., are they *POV shots*)? If so, what does the angle convey about that character's state of mind? If not, what does it convey about the person or thing in the frame?

What can I note about the composition of shots within a scene? Are the compositions balanced in a way that conforms to the so-called "rule of thirds," or are the elements within the frame arranged in a less "painterly" composition? How does the composition contribute to the scene overall?

Have the colors of a shot or scene been artificially manipulated through the use of color filters, different film stocks, or chemical or digital manipulation in order to create a mood or indicate a state of mind? What effect is achieved?

Does the cinematography ever call attention to itself? Is this a mistake or misjudgment on the filmmaker's part, or is it intentional? If intentional, what purpose is served by making the cinematography so noticeable?

Acting

Acting can encompass everything from an actor's performance in a movie to the aura of a movie star's persona in a film. The look, voice, gestures, and interpretation of a character by an actor can contribute enormously to a film's effect on the viewer. And as styles of acting have evolved over more than a century since the movies began, the analysis of acting is dependent on when a film was made, too. The following questions can help to guide your response to the acting in a movie:

Why was this actor, and not another, cast for the role?

Does the actor's performance create a coherent, unified character? If so, how?

Does the actor look the part? Is it necessary for the actor to look the part? Why or why not?

What elements are most distinctive in how the actor conveys the character's thoughts and internal complexities: body language, gestures, facial expressions, language? Did the actor use these elements successfully?

Does the actor seem to work well with fellow actors in this film? Put another way, is there chemistry? How do the actors make us feel that chemistry? Conversely, do any of the actors detract from the lead actor's performance?

Does the actor's performance have the expressive power to make me forget that he or she is acting? If so, how did the actor achieve this effect? If the actor is a movie star like Jennifer Lawrence, do I forget that I am watching Jennifer Lawrence, or am I acutely aware that this is a Jennifer Lawrence movie? What are the implications either way?

Editing

Editing is the process of selecting, arranging, and assembling the essential components of a movie—visual, sound, and special effects—to tell a film's story. It creates relationships between different shots and between the components of a shot, and from these relationships a film's meaning emerges. The different types and pacing of edits a filmmaker can make, from flashbacks, montages, rapid cuts or long tracking shots, jump cuts, cross-cutting, and more, contribute enormously to how we perceive a movie and its story. By asking some of the following questions, you can assess the effectiveness of editing in a film:

Does the movie's editing manipulate my experience of time? Is this condensing, slowing, speeding, repeating, or reordering of time simply practical (as in removing insignificant events), or is it expressive (in that it creates another layer of meaning)? If the play with time is expressive, just what is being expressed?

Does the editing overall seem to create continuity or discontinuity? If the editing is mostly creating continuity, are there nonetheless moments when the editing creates discontinuity? What is the significance of those moments?

What kind of transitions am I seeing from shot to shot or from scene to scene (e.g., types of cuts, dissolves, wipes, etc.)? Does the editor use one transitional effect more than others? Are the transitions seamless and nearly unnoticeable, or do they call attention to themselves? Why does the editor use these techniques? What is their effect?

As each shot cuts to the next shot in the scene or sequence, I'll tap my finger to get a feeling for the pace of the editing. How might I describe that pace? Does it stay constant, or does it speed up or slow down? How do rhythmic shifts and patterns affect mood and meaning?

Do any shots seem to be cut before I can fully absorb the content of the shot? Do any shots stay on screen long after I'm instinctively ready to move on to the next shot? How does deviating from a standard approach to duration change the way that I experience and interpret the shot?

Considering the different types of match cuts in the film, what visual or narrative information is each match cut conveying?

Do I see any moments in the movie in which the traditional conventions of Hollywood continuity editing—including use of the master shot, the 180-degree system, shot/reverse shot, match cuts, and parallel editing—are violated in some way? Where and how do these moments appear onscreen? What is the significance of these moments?

Sound

The sound we hear in a film—its music, dialogue, and sound effects—creates meaning just as much as what we see. Sound helps the filmmaker tell a movie's story by reproducing and intensifying the world that has been partially created by the film's visual elements. The choices made for dialogue, music, ambient sounds, and even silence can alter our impression of a scene completely, even if the visuals we see remain the same. Elements to consider when analyzing a film's sound include:

Which sounds are diegetic sounds? Which are nondiegetic? Which are onscreen sounds and which are offscreen sounds?

What types of sound (vocal sounds, ambient sounds, sound effects, music, silence) are used in this shot or scene? To what effect?

Are there moments when the sound creates emphasis by accentuating and strengthening the visual image? What is the purpose of this use of sound?

How does the sound develop characterization?

How is music used? In a complementary way? Ironically? Is the music nondiegetic, or are the characters within the shot or scene able to hear it?

Do image and sound complement one another in this movie, or does one dominate the other?

Does this film use silence expressively? How so?

In this movie, do I hear evidence of a comprehensive approach to sound—one, specifically, in which the film's sound is as expressive as its images? If so, what's going on?

Exploring Meaning

FORM AND CONTENT

Even though we've been spending a great deal of time asking you to consider a movie's formal elements, it's important for us to acknowledge that there is another aspect of any movie that goes hand in hand with its form, a component that shapes and is shaped by form, namely the movie's *content*.

The terms *form* and *content* crop up in almost any scholarly discussion of the arts. But what do they mean, and why are they so often paired? At the most basic level, we can define content as the subject of an artwork (what the work is about), and form as the means by which that subject is expressed and experienced. The two terms are often paired because works of art need them both. Content provides something to express; form supplies the methods and techniques necessary to present content to the audience.

However, form doesn't just allow us to *see* the subject/content; it lets us see that content *in a particular way*. Form enables the artist to shape both our experience and our interpretation of that content. As we try to understand how the movie we're analyzing *works*, we thus become more aware of how form and content interplay to make *meaning*. In other words, we come to see *form as content*, in that formal elements convey something important about content. We come to see *content as form*, in that content is shaped by the form it takes.

Complicating the matter further is that, in addition to the story that any movie tells, there are cultural values, shared ideals, and other ideas that lie just below the surface of that movie. These cultural contents—the story, the assumptions, the values, the ideas—as well as the particular form they take, create various layers of meaning within the movie. These layers of meaning overlap, intersect, and inform one another. The notion that any movie contains layers upon layers of meaning may make the process of looking at movies seem intimidating. But you'll find that the process of observing, identifying, and interpreting a movie's meanings will become considerably less mysterious once you grow accustomed to actively looking at movies rather than just watching them. It might also help to keep in mind that, no matter how many different layers of meaning there may be in a movie, each layer is either *explicit* or *implicit*.

EXPLICIT AND IMPLICIT MEANING

By explicit meaning, we mean a message that the movie presents right on its surface. The central facts of a story, for instance, are explicit. An implicit meaning, by contrast, lies below the surface of a movie's story and presentation, and is closest to our everyday sense of the word *meaning*. In this sense, implicit meaning is an association, connection, or inference that a viewer makes on the basis of the explicit meanings available on the surface of the film.

To tease out the difference between these two levels of meaning, let's look at two statements about *Juno* (2007). First, let's imagine that a friend who hasn't seen the movie asks us what the film is about. Our friend doesn't want a detailed plot summary; she simply wants to know what she'll see if she decides to watch the film. In other words, she is asking us for a statement about *Juno*'s explicit meaning. We might respond to her question by explaining: "The movie's about a rebellious but smart sixteen-year-old girl who gets pregnant and resolves to tackle the problem head-on. At first, she decides to get an abortion. But after she backs off that choice, she gets the idea of finding a couple to adopt the kid after it's born. She spends the rest of the movie dealing with the implications of that choice."

Now what if our friend hears this statement of explicit meaning and asks, "Okay, sure, but what do you think the movie is trying to say? What does it *mean*?" In a case like this, when someone is asking about the meaning of an entire film, he or she is seeking something like the film's overall message or "point." In essence, our friend is asking us to *interpret* the movie—to say something arguable about it—not simply to make a statement of obvious surface meaning that everyone can agree on. In other words, she is asking us for our sense of the movie's implicit meaning. One possible response might be: "A teenager faced with a difficult decision makes a bold leap toward adulthood but, in doing so, discovers that the world of adults is no less uncertain or overwhelming than adolescence."

At first glance, this statement might seem to have a lot in common with our summary of the movie's explicit meaning—as, of course, it does. After all, even though a meaning is under the surface, it nonetheless has to relate to the surface. Our interpretation of the film's implicit meaning therefore needs to be grounded in the surface's explicitly presented details. Nevertheless, if you compare the two statements closely, you can see that the second one is more interpretive than the first, more concerned with what the movie "means."

Explicit and implicit meanings need not pertain to the movie as a whole, and not all implicit meaning is tied to broad messages or themes. Smaller doses of both kinds of meaning are present in virtually every scene. For example, Juno's application of lipstick before she visits the adoptive father, Mark, is explicit information. The meaning of this action—that her admiration for Mark is beginning to develop into something approaching a crush—is implicit. Later, Mark's announcement that he is leaving his wife and does not want to be a father sends Juno into a panicked retreat. On her drive home, a crying jag forces the disillusioned Juno to pull off the highway. She skids to a stop beside a rotting boat abandoned in a ditch. The discarded boat's decayed condition and the incongruity of a watercraft adrift in an expanse of grass are explicit details that convey implicit meaning about Juno's isolation and alienation. In the end, our ability to understand and appreciate the film depends on our ability to make the associations between its explicit and implicit messages.

4

Cultural Analysis

As we've already said, filmmakers use the conventions of cinematic language to make the inner workings of a movie "invisible" to us as viewers. They want us to be immersed in the imaginative world they've created, not distracted by the technical mechanisms that they've employed to create that world.

The same commercial instinct that inspires filmmakers to hide their methods and mechanisms from our view also compels them to favor stories and themes that reinforce viewers' shared belief systems. For the most part, the mainstream film industry seeks to entertain, not to provoke, its customers. A key to entertaining one's customers is to "give them what they want"—to tap into and reinforce their most fundamental desires and beliefs. Even movies deemed "controversial" or "provocative" can be popular if they trigger emotional responses from their viewers that reinforce yearnings or beliefs that lie deep within. Because so much of this response occurs on an unconscious, emotional level, the casual viewer may be blind to the implied political, cultural, and ideological messages that help to make the movie so appealing.

Of course, this cultural invisibility is not always a calculated decision on the part of the filmmakers. Directors, screenwriters, and producers are, after all, products of the same society inhabited by their intended audience. Oftentimes, the people making the movies may be just as oblivious of the cultural attitudes shaping their cinematic stories as the people who watch them.

Thus, the layers of implicit meaning in any film include not only those that the filmmakers have consciously crafted, but also those that they have not intended. This fact can be liberating for you as you write about film: you are not limited to deciphering the filmmaker's intent but can explore the unintended messages of the film, as well as the effect the film has on its audiences. Having taken this time to explain what we mean when we talk about "meaning," we can now turn to the next general approach to film analysis: *cultural analysis*.

What Is Cultural Analysis?

Scholars of cinema look not only at the surface of a film to understand how it "works"; they also examine the layers of implicit meaning that reflect any cultural assumptions that the filmmakers and audience might take for granted.

The tools that scholars use to analyze films in this manner are borrowed from critical theories first developed by social theorists, cultural critics, and philosophers. While these theoretical perspectives are the "tools of the trade" for professional scholars of film, they can prove challenging to students who are just beginning their studies. You needn't feel pressured to master film theory before writing your paper. Even a basic understanding of the theoretical perspectives commonly used by film scholars can be useful to novice writers. First, these theories can show you how to cast a more analytical eye on the unspoken assumptions and ideals that seem to be taken for granted in the movies you write about. Second, these theories can be used to jump-start a paper by giving you different frames through which you can view a film.

The most important theoretical frames in film studies include *Marxism*, *feminism*, *race and ethnicity studies*, and *queer theory*. When applied to film, these perspectives offer a critical lens through which you can examine a movie's portrayal of socioeconomic status (Marxism), gender (feminism), racial, ethnic, or national identities (race and ethnicity studies), and sexual orientation (queer theory). Let's look at each of these categories to see how they might serve your film analyses.

SOCIOECONOMIC STATUS

The stories that human beings tell each other cannot avoid issues of socioeconomic status. Characters are rich, or poor, or somewhere in between, and the concrete realities of their existence determine both the way they are developed as characters and the challenges the narrative throws their way.

Depending on the filmmaker's perspective and the culture in which the film is made and screened, a movie can portray a particular social class negatively, approvingly, or anywhere in between. The film may offer explicit or implied messages about the rightness (or wrongness) of the social hierarchies portrayed onscreen. Or, it may seem as though the filmmakers and the characters are willfully blind to the tensions that exist across and among various socioeconomic classes.

The theoretical perspective that concerns itself with issues of socioeconomic class in cinema is *Marxist film analysis*. This framework focuses on the ways that movies either reinforce or undermine the dominant power structures in a society. Based on the extensive philosophical/economic writings of Karl Marx (1818–1883), this form of theoretical analysis sees movies not as innocent entertainment, but rather as an important means by which the social status quo is either maintained (most of the time) or disrupted (occasionally).

Marx himself saw the arts (along with law, religion, and other institutions) as part of the *superstructure* of society—an overlay of ideas and ideologies that reflects the perspective of those at the highest levels of power. According to Marx, popular art forms (including movies) typically lure the working classes and the poor to rally around the ideas that perpetuate the power of those at the very top of the social ladder. When there is broad consensus among the working classes and the poor that the status quo, while unfair to them, is inevitable and proper, then they are exhibiting, to use Marx's phrase, "false consciousness." The values they subscribe to are working directly against their socioeconomic interests. In Marx's view, popular art is one of the means by which the powerful lure the poor and working classes to embrace false consciousness, and to internalize the dominant culture's values and ideas.

Of course, any work of art may work against some aspects of the dominant power structure even as it buttresses others. There is always the potential for works of art to break free of the dominant narrative and to introduce perspectives that inspire us to see "the way things are" with fresh eyes. Nevertheless, according to this theory, the very powerful pull of one's social milieu prevents even the most radical artist from breaking entirely free from accepted ideas and expressions.

Following this line of thinking, many contemporary film scholars examine movies to uncover their unspoken ideas about power and class. Marxist analysis examines the ways that social classes are represented in a film, as well as what messages the film seems to be sending about each class and its place in the hierarchy. When looking at films that set out specifically to undercut the dominant ideology, Marxist analysis examines both the ways that the film succeeds in doing so, and the ways that it inadvertently reinforces existing social structures.

If you are interested in considering issues of socioeconomic status as a springboard for your analysis, you might consider asking the following questions:

Does the socioeconomic status of each character play a significant role in the narrative? How so?

Are people from a particular class portrayed negatively (or positively) in this movie? If so, what seems to be the point of that portrayal?

Does this film seem to set out to critique the socioeconomic status quo? In what ways does it do so? What aspects of the status quo does it leave unquestioned?

Is nearly everything of value in this movie something that can be bought and sold (i.e., a *commodity*)? Or does the film portray values that fall outside the realm of economics? Overall, what values are being argued for in this film? How is this argument being presented?

Since the movies began, money has been a favorite subject in countless gangster movies, as well as such films as *Greed* (1924; director Erich von Stroheim), *Citizen Kane* (1941; Orson Welles), *There Will Be Blood* (2007; Paul Thomas Anderson), and *All the Money in the World* (2017; Ridley Scott). Money motivates both men and women from all races, creeds, and backgrounds. That's no surprise in the United States, a country that prizes entrepreneurship and success.

Interestingly, movies about sports often concern the role that money and socioeconomic status play in winning. Take, for example, *The Color of Money* (1986; director Martin Scorsese), *Raging Bull* (1980; Martin Scorsese), or *Jerry Maguire* (1996; Cameron Crowe). *Foxcatcher* (2014; Bennett Miller) is another. It's about the particular (some would say peculiar) desire of a real-life character, John du Pont (Steve Carell), to spend whatever amount it takes to create a U.S. wrestling team for the Olympics. For du Pont, an heir to one of the world's largest fortunes, this seems easy, even a foregone conclusion. So, with stubborn determination and substantial financial incentives, he recruits a group that includes brothers Mark and Dave Schultz (Channing Tatum and Mark Ruffalo, respectively), star wrestlers from the opposite end of the socioeconomic scale. Here, old money = power, while young wrestlers = talent. It is a story that begins with promises of glory and ends in tragedy when du Pont murders Dave, seemingly out of jealousy, because Dave has the admiration of his brother, as well as a loving wife and children.

In a movie where money is so important, socioeconomic forces might have been responsible, at least in part, for this ending. Is du Pont's money more important than the sport he loves? Does money buy happiness? Is money the "root of all evil"? Does money corrupt sports? Is du Pont portrayed as evil? Are the needy boys portrayed as vulnerable commodities being used for du Pont's dreams of glory? To what extent does money define a family's values? What is the difference, if any, between du Pont's legendary "dynasty" and the Schultzes' developing sports dynasty?

GENDER

Like socioeconomic status, gender is a part of every story ever told. In fact, most of the world's most popular stories hinge on some aspect of gender—whether the story is about what it means to be a man or a woman, or the often fraught relations between the sexes, or the social roles that are traditionally assigned to one gender or another.

The theoretical lens through which these issues are analyzed by film scholars is *feminism* (or *gender studies*). Feminist film theory brings to the study of movies the same overall concerns that mark the feminist movement as a whole: a desire for equality with men, in society and in the arts; a critical examination of the roles that women have traditionally been expected to fill in society; and a sensitivity to (and critical perspective on) the representations of women and men that reinforce stereotypes and that make the status quo seem "natural" and inevitable.

Feminist film critics have focused their attention particularly on representations of women as passive objects of male desire. Such portrayals back female characters into a corner where their very identities are defined primarily by men, who either validate them or reject them based on their sexual attractiveness. But even more interestingly, we, members of the audience—whether we're male or female—do so as well. In her landmark essay, "Visual Pleasure and Narrative Cinema" (1975), the film scholar Laura Mulvey takes the position that movies lure audiences to identify with the male protagonist's (and the camera's) "gaze," and to thereby judge the worth of the female character as we would any beautiful object to be looked at (i.e., based on desirability).

There are other traditional "types" of female characters in art, of course—the virginal naïf, the helpless "damsel in distress," the femme fatale, etc.—but these, too, according to feminist critics, have their origins in prejudicial stereotypes constructed by and for men. A core task of feminist critique, therefore, is to identify and to deconstruct these stereotyped portrayals wherever and whenever they appear in the movies.

Because of the work of feminist critics at least since the 1960s, women are now producing more films, and otherwise influencing the portrayals of women onscreen, than they ever have before. Some feminist critics are therefore devoting at least part of their efforts to writing about filmmakers whose work breaks with past stereotypes, portraying women in less passive, more diverse and fully realized ways. These critics advocate on behalf of films that are more nuanced in their portrayal of gender.

If you are interested in investigating how gender plays out in movies, here are a few questions you can ask yourself to jump-start your thinking:

Are the main female characters in this movie as fully realized as the male characters? What characteristics do the female characters possess? Which do they lack? What does this tell us about how the filmmakers are positioning women?

Is the identity of the main female character (or characters) defined primarily by her (or their) sex appeal? What are the implications of this portrayal?

Does this movie's narrative seem to suggest that the relations between the sexes are "natural" and proper, or does it seem to critique the status quo? If the latter, what is the nature of the critique?

Does this film reflect or work against the assumptions about gender roles that prevailed at the time when this movie was made and screened? How so?

Do the formal aspects of this movie (the cinematography, the editing, etc.) cause you to see the female characters from the perspective of a male protagonist? In what way does this perspective limit your understanding of the characters?

Do you find yourself sympathizing with the main female character(s) in this film? Why or why not?

Although worldwide feminist movements hold at least one objective in common—equality for women and men—there are countries where women have responsibilities unique to their society, ones that do not always involve equality. We see this in *Fill the Void* (2012), director Rama Burshtein's intimately observed drama about a predicament faced by an Orthodox Hasidic family in Israel. The title refers to the challenge faced by Yochay (Yiftach Klein), whose wife, Esther, dies in childbirth and leaves him with the dilemma of what to do about raising their baby. An observant Jew (as are all the characters), he understands the rigid rules and traditions by which this ancient community lives, including arranged marriages. In almost every way, the men and women lead very different lives from one another. The director, an affirmed feminist, shows that however disturbing the practice of arranged marriage may be to some audiences, the woman has the final choice of whom she will marry, even though she is presented with many obstacles in reaching her decision. *Fill the Void* was released to audiences both inside and outside the Orthodox community.

In "filling the void," which suggests a mechanical rather than a meaningful way to find a new wife, Yochay has two choices: marry his 18-year-old sister-in-law, Shira Mendelman (Hadas Yaron)—who has already been looking after the child but is hoping for an arranged marriage with a young man she likes—or an older woman in Belgium whom he has known since childhood but who does not appear in the film. It is not an easy choice for him, and there is no shortage of advice from family, rabbinical elders, and busybodies about what he (and Shira) should do. To some, it would appear that there is only room in this community for tradition, obligation, and interference, but not for love.

Indeed, Yochay and Shira have many serious discussions about their reasons for marrying, but neither mentions love. In this confusion, each is hurt in one way or another by selfishness, misread intentions, and masked emotions. Finally, after much thought, ritual, and prayer, love seems to transfigure both of them, but still neither says the word. The director deliberately leaves the interpretation to us. It is a feeling, not a fact. Nonetheless, the decision to marry is Shira's, and hers alone. They marry, and the film ends as they enter their new apartment.

The movie gives us sufficient information about this community to enable us to study the dilemma as we see it and reach some opinions of our own about the role that gender plays in it. The challenge is to understand, not to judge. In this process, you might consider the following:

Has the process of thought, discussion, and decision changed Shira? If so, how?

Outside of the relatively closed community in which Shira lives, is she a recognizable female character?

Is her character development believable? Or is she a sterotype?

The director is female. From what perspective does she portray the characters, both male and female? In particular, does she photograph the women differently from the men?

Regardless of your gender, do you sympathize with the women and men in the film, and Shira and Yochay in particular?

At the end of the movie, Yochay shuts the door of their new apartment while Shira stands timidly. Does this door have symbolic value in relation to their new life together?

Shira is a young woman in a closed community with a fixed way of life, but we also see that the larger society outside is changing culturally. Does her age give her an advantage in dealing with her decision?

RACE, ETHNICITY, AND NATIONAL ORIGIN

Many films in the long history of American cinema present only (or primarily) white characters onscreen. Others have a diverse cast of characters but present racial or ethnic minorities in a mildly unflattering, or even blatantly prejudicial, manner. In contemporary cinema, the perspectives of people of various racial, ethnic, and national origins are very much present, more than they have ever been before. And yet mainstream Hollywood movies, even now, often stumble into caricature and stereotypical representations of people whose race, ethnicity, or place of origin differs from what the producers of those movies assume are their primary audience.

When societies are composed of a majority population that shares certain characteristics, real or imagined, there is a tendency to privilege that majority's perspective. The perspectives of minority populations are either ignored or "othered," thereby asserting the superiority of the majority group and its values. Such beliefs make it difficult for members of any other group to be seen, heard, or treated with respect.

Film scholars and critics who are sensitive to these issues bring a wide range of analytical and theoretical tools to their work, so it's difficult to give a name to some specific theoretical perspective that these critics adopt when they write about film. Professional criticism about cultural portrayals of race, ethnicity, and origin generally depends on a wide familiarity with core concepts in psychology, sociology, and philosophy, and on a broad understanding of cultural and political history.

For beginning students of film, a sensitivity to the relevant issues (or a direct experience of having been viewed as an "other") can enrich any analysis of a movie that portrays tensions or imbalances across the boundaries of race, ethnicity, or national origin. Merely asking pointed questions about these movies can lead you to observations that add significant interest and weight to your analysis. Here are a few questions you might ask to get yourself started.

Given what you know about the place or time portrayed in the movie, are there groups of people not shown or barely acknowledged in the movie who were nonetheless significant and visible there and then? Why do you think they aren't portrayed in this movie?

Does the movie use visual cues—in lighting, camera angles, editing decisions, costume, makeup, or actors' gestures—to establish that a character or a group of characters is clearly an "other"—a strange, foreign, or menacing type of person who falls outside of the "normal" majority? If so, what are the cues and how do they work?

Is the movie seemingly content to reinforce traditional stereotypes of minority characters? Or does it seem to be working against them? How so?

Does the movie portray racial, ethnic, or cross-cultural relations as complex and contradictory social interactions? Or does the film offer, literally and figuratively, a "black-and-white" worldview? What is the effect of the complex or simplistic portrayal of these relations?

With today's national concerns about race, law enforcement, and immigration laws, we see American movies attempting to deal seriously and honestly with the subjects of race, ethnicity, and national origin, including (to name a few) *Django Unchained* (2012; Quentin Tarantino), *Fruitvale Station* (2013; Ryan Coogler), *12 Years a Slave* (2013; Steve McQueen), *Lee Daniels' The Butler* (2013; Lee Daniels), *Selma* (2014; Ava DuVernay), and Hidden Figures (2016; Theodore Melfi). These films depict slavery, the civil rights movement, and domestic situations that were largely ignored throughout American film history. And their directors, both white and black, depict racial, ethnic, or cross-cultural interactions with multiple perspectives. To be sure, a film like *12 Years a Slave* represents a black-and-white worldview of evil white plantation owners versus victimized black slaves, but it also provides other perspectives, including those of whites opposed to slavery, and blacks who betray each other.

Tate Taylor's *The Help* (2011) presents a dense tangle of stories, at the heart of which is a clear-eyed, level-headed examination of how white women treated their black female servants ("the help") in 1960s Jackson, Mississippi, one of the most troubled spots in the South. These middle-class white women have little to do besides host card parties and boss around their black servants, who not only do all their domestic chores but also care for their children. The movie depicts the racism of this little town so thoroughly that we understand that these women have never known any way of life apart from white supremacy. But there are exceptions. Eugenia "Skeeter" Phelan (Emma Stone), a young white woman, returns from college and encourages the maids to tell their stories for a book she is compiling. When it is published, it exposes their employers and blows the town wide open. Two other white women, long ingrained in the town's culture, are strong enough to change their attitudes: Skeeter's mother (Allison Janney) changes almost too late, but the mother (Sissy Spacek) of the film's most obnoxious hostess has long opposed her daughter's behavior. The leading black characters (Viola Davis, Octavia Spencer, and Cicely Tyson) must behave as their employers demand, but they do not reinforce stereotypes of black servants. We see the impact of the town's low wages, hard discipline, segregated buses and housing, and reduced educational opportunities on these women and their families. And in both the black and white communities, the director shoots with an almost documentary precision to show us how each side lives, never exaggerating or simplifying to make a point. It's as if we are there, seeing it with our own eyes, and it has to be that way, for most of us have never experienced firsthand a town like Jackson. Taylor's approach makes it very difficult not to trust his vision.

The Help depicts a place and time that we know is still deeply flawed in its racial attitudes, and its characters, both black and white, are shown honestly. It is primarily a film about women, and the decor of their homes, as well as their appearance, speech patterns, and manners, clearly distinguish between the leisure and working classes. Although the movie ends on a hopeful note, we know that however accurate its depictions may be (and not all would agree on this point), it has presented a world that heretofore Hollywood has peopled with stereotypes, often comic nannies and maids.

SEXUAL ORIENTATION

When it comes to human sexuality, what is "normal"? What is "deviant"? There's no question that these categories are of great interest to many people, and that public attitudes about the boundaries between the various categories of sexual practice are always in flux.

Scholars who critique movie portrayals of "deviant" sexualities or who look critically at the tendency in mainstream cinema to reinforce the idea that heterosexuality is the sole "normal" variety of human sexual identity use a broad array of theoretical tools to conduct their analyses. The umbrella that encompasses all of this work is often called "queer theory."

Film scholars who use queer theory as their lens of analysis focus their attention on cinematic portrayals of alternative sexualities and on the various ways that movies convey "heteronormative" messages (i.e., the subtle or not-so-subtle messages that support the view that only heterosexuality deserves to be considered "normal"). These scholars are often interested in presentations of transgressive phenomena such as drag, cross-dressing, camp, and transsexuality, chiefly because these phenomena cast in high relief the conventions of gender that are clearly "performative" and therefore easily (and often quite entertainingly) parodied. Another obvious task of queer theory is to critique omissions, distortions, and stereotypes of alternative sexual identities wherever they appear.

It's interesting to note that many film artists throughout history who were gay, lesbian, transgender, or otherwise outside the societally defined "norm" of sexual identity have kept this aspect of their identity under wraps. Queer theorists often uncover or make more apparent the fact of these filmmakers' sexual identities, analyzing the ways that their films reflect (or conceal) their identities.

If you're interested in analyzing a film through the lens of sexual orientation or identity, you might begin by asking the following questions:

Does the movie present a straightforward and uncomplicated portrait of heterosexual relationships? Or does it introduce narrative elements that portray alternative sexual identities? In either case, what comments about sexuality is the film making?

If the movie does portray alternative sexualities, does it present people as social deviants, as comic foils, or as otherwise "abnormal" characters? Or are these characters portrayed as fully realized human beings?

If a movie seems primarily occupied with portraying heterosexuality as the norm to be emulated and celebrated, does it nonetheless contain subtle narrative or visual elements which undermine that portrait of normalcy? What are these elements, and how are they in play?

What function, if any, do performative aspects of gender and sexuality have in the film? Are there camp elements? Drag? Cross-dressing? Are they meant to be merely laughed at or dismissed as deviant, or do they move the movie's narrative in an interesting direction?

If you watch a film made by or starring a film artist who was eventually revealed to be gay, lesbian, bisexual, transgender, or of some other alternative sexual identity, what aspects of the film seem to flow from this identity, and which aspects seem to contradict it?

We have long passed the time when homosexuality was a taboo subject in popular culture. Indeed, the word *homosexuality* has given way to the acronym LGBT (lesbian, gay, bisexual, and transgender), although it is not completely inclusive of the varieties of sexual orientation and expression that currently exist. The subject is out of the closet and widely represented in books, theater, music, television shows, and movies. In the past decade, there have been more feature movies dealing with LGBT issues than we can easily list here, and that does not include documentaries, avant-garde, or animated films. Among other issues, these films deal with parental and societal discrimination, the coming-out process, and the actions and attitudes of all concerned. They represent a cross-section of LGBT characters and societies in countries both East and West—including England, France, Germany, Israel, Arab states, the United States, Japan, Hong Kong, Taiwan, South Korea, Thailand, the Philippines, and India—although the primary focus to date has been on gay men. They are both ordinary men (real and fictional) and politicians (Harvey Milk), writers (Truman Capote), artists (Francis Bacon), athletes (Glenn Burke), and celebrities (Liberace). Among the feature films about lesbians are *Go Fish* (1994; director Rose Troche), *Heavenly Creatures* (1994; Peter Jackson), *Kissing Jessica Stein* (2002; Charles Herman-Wurmfeld), *Monster* (2003; Patty Jenkins), *The Kids Are All Right* (2010; Lisa Cholodenko), and *Blue Is the Warmest Color* (2013; Abdellatif Kechiche). The characters in these films represent a rich spectrum of race, gender, ethnicity, religion, and sexual orientation. And their stories have been told in all genres, whether drama, melodrama, or comedy, true or fictional.

Some of these movies have reached a wide audience, while others have appealed to more specialized groups. But the one movie about sexual orientation that almost everyone knows is Jean-Marc Vallée's *Dallas Buyers Club* (2013), which tells a true story about gay and transgender Texans in the 1980s and the

AIDS epidemic. (The first major film about AIDS was Jonathan Demme's *Philadelphia* [1993].) The movie vividly depicts the Dallas gay scene—not only the drinking, drug abuse, casual sex, and rowdy clubs, but more importantly the devastating effects of the HIV virus before antiviral drugs were developed to treat it. It had wide exposure and won Academy Awards for Matthew McConaughey as Best Actor (Ron Woodruff) and Jared Leto as Best Supporting Actor (Rayon).

Woodruff, once a loud, violent homophobe, learns that he has AIDS, and channels all his energy into importing the drug AZT and selling it to the afflicted. He is initially hostile toward Rayon, a drug-addicted, HIV-positive transgender woman, who eventually joins him in running the buyers club. Rayon, who is a delightful and thoughtful contrast to Woodruff, dies during the course of the movie; an onscreen note informs us that Woodruff died in 1992, but not before playing a significant role in convincing the Food and Drug Administration to test and approve the first antiviral drugs.

The challenge in writing about this movie is not the story, but rather the director's vision and the performances of the two leading actors. Various directors (and actors) were considered before the final choices were made. Jean-Marc Vallée was chosen as director, perhaps because his film *C.R.A.Z.Y.* (2005), based on his own experiences, depicts a young man dealing with homophobia. An interesting array of actors was considered before final casting of McConaughey and Leto. Both play characters who are extreme in their respective appearances and attitudes, and each is larger than life in his own way: Woodruff is very theatrical in his attempts to help his fellow men, and Rayon brings color, humor, and reason to a character who has nothing to lose. Both actors lost about 50 pounds in order to look convincing as people dying from AIDS.

The LGBT world encompasses many types of people and behavior, some of which have become stereotyped through the mass media. But the film is set exclusively in Dallas in the late 1980s, a long time before the more recent successes achieved by the gay rights movement. The more familiar you are with the LGBT world and its citizens, the easier it will be for you to write about this movie.

Whatever your perspectives on the LGBT world, you will need to determine for yourself the director's perspective in telling the story and directing the actors. How does the director visually depict the city, citizens, and health-care system of Dallas? Does he present the operators or patrons of the buyers club as deviants or stereotypes? The buyers club depicted in the movie is a humanitarian effort that operates outside the law. Does this status affect your thinking about it? And you would need to determine the effectiveness with which the two leading actors play their roles. Leto's appearance as Rayon involves an elaborate transformative look (the film won a third Academy Award for makeup and hairstyle). How does this affect your interpretation of the character? Does McConaughey make a convincing change from a stereotyped villain to a studious and effective activist? Is he believable in the role?

Genre Study

Film scholars may analyze a movie based on a wide range of criteria, including its specific aesthetic style, the artists who created it, its country or region of origin, its apparent ideologies, or the cinematic movement from which it emerged. But one of the most enduring criteria that has determined how movies are studied and analyzed is *genre*—the categorization of narrative films by the stories that they tell and the ways they tell them.

Commonly recognized movie genres include westerns, horror films, science fiction, musicals, and gangster films. But this list is far from complete. The film industry also produces action movies, biographies (biopics), melodramas, thrillers, romances, romantic comedies, fantasy films, and many others that fall within some genre or subgenre.

Whether or not your paper focuses on a film's genre, nearly any kind of film analysis will benefit from an awareness of it. Understanding some basic principles about film genres, and about their importance in the film industry and in film scholarship, will help you develop interesting critiques even if your analysis is primarily about some other aspect of the movie(s) you are analyzing.

THE EMERGENCE OF FILM GENRES

Unlike film movements (such as French New Wave or Dogme 95), in which a group of like-minded filmmakers conspire to create a particular approach to film style and story, film genres tend to spring up organically—not through any conscious plan, but rather because of a cultural need to explore and express certain ideas. Cultural conditions inspire artists to tell certain kinds of stories, the nature of which motivates certain technical and aesthetic approaches. Eventually the accumulation of like-minded movies is detected, labeled, studied, and explicated by cinema scholars.

Of course, academic scholars are not the only movie lovers who find it useful to categorize films by genre. Genre has a significant effect on how audiences choose the movies they attend, rent, or purchase. Genre films have been prevalent since the earliest days of cinema because, contrary to popular perceptions, most movie viewers value predictability over novelty. Elements of certain genres appeal to us, so we seek to repeat an entertaining or engaging cinema experience by viewing a film that promises the same surefire ingredients. We get a certain pleasure from seeing how different filmmakers and performers have rearranged and interpreted familiar elements. We also enjoy seeing how a filmmaker or performer might deviate from the usual path. To put this relationship into gastronomic terms: the most common pizza features a flour-based crust topped with tomato sauce and mozzarella cheese, but it's the potential variety within that familiar foundation that has made pizza one of America's favorite foods.

A less obvious explanation for the persistent prevalence of genre lies in the deep roots genre has in our society. Any given genre naturally emerges not because Hollywood thinks it'll sell, but because it gives narrative voice to something essential to our culture. The film industry may ultimately exploit our love of certain genres, but it's our interests in certain kinds of movies that create genres in the first place. No studio executive decided (for instance) to invent horror movies out of thin air. Rather, these films exist because of our collective fear of death and the human psyche's need for catharsis. Westerns endorse ideas about America that Americans need to believe. We go to these movies not only to celebrate the familiar, but to enforce fundamental beliefs. As our world evolves and audience perspectives change, genre movies adapt to reflect these cultural shifts. A western made during the can-do patriotism of World War II is likely to express its themes differently than one produced at the height of the Vietnam War.

PREDICTABILITY AND INNOVATION

Once a particular genre has crystallized, then of course Hollywood executives use the newly emergent category to help them decide which projects to bankroll. Genres, once recognized and defined, offer familiar story formulas, conventions, themes, and conflicts, as well as immediately recognizable visual icons, all of which together provide a blueprint for creating and marketing a type of film that has proven successful in the past. Studios and distributors can develop genre-identified stars, select directors on the basis of proven proficiency in a particular genre, piggyback on the success of a previous genre hit, and even recycle props, sets, costumes, and digital backgrounds. Just as important, the industry counts on genre to predict ticket sales, to pre-sell markets, and to cash in on recent trends by making films that allow consumers to predict they'll like a particular movie. In other words, give people what they want, and they will buy it. This simple economic principle helps us to understand the phenomenal growth of the movie industry from the 1930s on, as well as the mind-numbing mediocrity of so many of the movies that the industry produces. The kind of strict adherence to genre convention driven solely by economics often yields derivative and formulaic results.

If genre films are prone to mediocrity, why are so many great filmmakers drawn to making them? The beginning of the answer can be found, of all places, in a statement by the Nobel Prize–winning poet T. S. Eliot, who wrote: "When forced to work within a strict framework, the imagination is taxed to its utmost—and will produce its richest ideas." Eliot was talking about poetry, but the same concept can be applied to cinema. Creatively ambitious writers and directors often challenge themselves to create art within the strict confines of genre convention. A genre's so-called rules can provide a foundation upon which the filmmaker can both honor traditions and innovate change. The resulting stories often fulfill some expectations while surprising and subverting others. Indeed, genre has intrigued so many of our greatest American and European filmmakers that many entries in the canon of important and transformative movies are genre films.

It should be clear by now that genre films provide lots of opportunities for interesting analyses. If you're convinced that grappling with a specific genre film or with a genre overall is something you'd like to do in your own writing, here are some basic principles of genre to keep in mind.

GENRE CONVENTIONS

Movie genres are defined by sets of conventions. These conventions include aspects of storytelling such as themes, situations, settings, character types, and story formula, as well as aspects of presentation such as decor, lighting, and sound. Even the movie stars associated with a particular genre can be considered one of these defining conventions. Keep in mind that these conventions are not enforced; filmmakers don't follow mandated genre checklists. While every movie within any particular genre will incorporate some of these elements, few genre movies attempt to include every possible genre convention.

Story Formulas. The way a movie's story is structured—its plot—also helps viewers determine what genre it belongs to.

For example, gangster films—from Howard Hawks's *Scarface* (1932) to Martin Scorsese's *The Irishman* (2019)—tend to share a plot structure in which an underprivileged and disrespected immigrant joins (or forms) an organized-crime syndicate, works his way to the top with a combination of savvy, innovation, and ruthlessness, becomes corrupted by his newfound power and the fruits of his labors, and as a result is betrayed, killed, or captured. Romantic-comedy plots are structured around characters in love as they couple, break up, and reconnect. When they first meet, the two characters (usually a man and a woman) are at odds. They fall in love in spite of—or sometimes because of—this seeming incompatibility, then must overcome obstacles to their relationship in the form of misunderstandings, competing partners, social pressures, or the aforementioned incompatibility. Eventually the romance will appear doomed, but one half of the couple will realize they are meant for each other and make a grand gesture that reunites the romantic duo.

Themes. A movie's *theme* is a unifying idea that the film expresses through its narrative or imagery. Not every genre is united by a single, clear-cut thematic idea, but the western comes close. Nearly all westerns share a central conflict between civilization and wilderness: settlers, towns, schoolteachers, cavalry outposts, and lawmen stand for civilization; free-range cattlemen, Indians, prostitutes, outlaws, and the wide-open spaces themselves fill the wilderness role. Many classic western characters exist on both sides of this conflict. For example, the Wyatt Earp character played by Henry Fonda in John Ford's *My Darling Clementine* (1946) is a former gunfighter turned lawman turned cowboy turned lawman. He befriends an outlaw but falls in love with a schoolteacher from the East. Early westerns tend to sympathize with the forces of civilization and order, but many of the westerns from the 1960s and 1970s valorize the freedom-loving outlaw, cowboy, or Native American hero.

Gangster films are shaped by three well-worn but obviously resonant themes that can each be summarized in a phrase: "rags to riches"; "crime does not pay"; and "absolute power corrupts absolutely." The thematic complexity made possible by the tension between these aspirational and moralistic ideas can provide the viewer with a more meaningful experience than one might expect from a genre dedicated to career criminals.

Character Types. While most screenwriters strive to create individuated characters, genre films are often populated by specific character "types." Western protagonists personify the tension between order and chaos in the form of the free-spirited but civilized cowboy, or the gunslinger turned lawman. Female characters also personify this tension, but only on one side or the other—as schoolmarm or prostitute, and only rarely as a combination of both. Other western character types include the cunning gambler, the greenhorn, the sidekick, and the settler. John Ford packed nearly every western character type into a single wagon in his classic western *Stagecoach* (1939). The horror and science fiction film antagonist is almost always some form of "other"—a being utterly different from the movie's protagonist (and audience) in form, attitude, and action. Many of these movie monsters look like large, malevolent bugs—the more foreign the villain's appearance and outlook the better. When the "other" is actually a human, he often wears a mask designed to accentuate his otherness.

Setting. Where a movie's action is located and how that environment is portrayed—otherwise known as *setting*—is also a common genre convention. Obviously, westerns are typically set in the American West, but setting goes beyond geography. Most classic westerns take place in the 1880s and 1890s, an era of western settlement when a booming population of Civil War veterans and other eastern refugees went west in pursuit of land, gold, and cattle trade. The physical location of Monument Valley became the landscape most associated with the genre, not because of any actual history that occurred there, but because the scenic area was the favorite location of the prolific western director John Ford. Since science fiction films are speculative, and therefore look forward rather than backward, they are usually set in the future: sometimes in space, sometimes in futuristic Earth cities, sometimes in a post-apocalyptic desolation, but almost always in an era and place greatly affected by technology. While gangster films are almost always urban in setting, horror films seek the sort of isolated locations—farms, abandoned summer camps, small rural villages—that place the genre's besieged protagonists far from potential aid.

Presentation / iconic imagery. Many genres feature elements of cinematic language that communicate tone and atmosphere and that viewers come to associate with those genres more than others.

Horror films take advantage of lighting schemes that accentuate and deepen shadows. While the resulting gloom helps to create an eerie mood, horror films are more than just dark; filmmakers use the hard-edged shadows as a dominant compositional element to convey a sense of oppression, to distort our sense of space, and to conceal narrative information. Film noir, a genre that also seeks to disorient the viewer and convey a sense of unease (although for very different thematic and narrative reasons), employs many of the same lighting techniques.

Westerns, a genre clearly associated with setting, feature a great many exterior shots that juxtapose the characters with the environment they inhabit. The human subject tends to dominate the frame in most movie compositions, but many of these western exterior shots are framed so that the "civilized" characters are dwarfed by the overwhelming expanse of wilderness around them.

Movies in the action genre often shoot combat (and other high-energy action) from many different angles to allow for a fast-paced editing style that presents the action from a constantly shifting perspective. These highly fragmented sequences subject the viewer to a rapid-fire cinematic simulation of the amplified experiences of the characters fighting onscreen.

Such iconic imagery often becomes so intimately entwined with a genre that when filmmakers later use these images, they signal either that they are making a joke, or that they are making an explicit homage to the original genre or to the particular filmmaker who pioneered the iconic imagery.

Stars. Even the actors who star in genre movies factor into how the genre is classified, analyzed, and received by audiences. In the 1930s and 1940s, actors worked under restrictive long-term studio contracts. With the studios choosing their roles, actors were more likely to be "typecast" and identified with a particular genre that suited their studio-imposed persona. Thus, John Wayne is forever identified with the western, Edward G. Robinson with gangster films, and Boris Karloff with horror. These days, most actors avoid limiting themselves to a single genre, but several contemporary actors have become stars by associating themselves almost exclusively with action films. Arnold Schwarzenegger, Chuck Norris, Steven Seagal, and others have benefited from the genre's preference for physical presence and macho persona over acting ability. That's not to say that genre stars can't act. In fact, an actor who has become identified with one genre will often receive extra attention and accolades for performing outside of it. For example, Bill Murray became a star while acting in screwball comedies, but his subtle performances in the dramas *Lost in Translation* (2003; director Sofia Coppola) and *Broken Flowers* (2005; Jim Jarmusch) made him an actor worthy of movie critics' praise.

EVOLUTION OF GENRES

As the major film genres have evolved, filmmakers working within them have begun to display greater self-consciousness of the history and conventions of genre. This development is visible in such simple touches as a brief reference or homage to a previous film. Consider, for instance, Wes Craven's *Scream* (1996), which self-consciously echoes, recasts, and parodies such classic horror films as Alfred Hitchcock's *Psycho* (1960), John Carpenter's *Halloween* (1978), and the horror genre itself.

The process of genre transformation is as organic as the process that sprouts new genres. Existing genres change with the times and adapt to audience expectations, which are in turn influenced by many factors—technological, cultural, social, political, economic, and so on. Arguably, genres that don't evolve lose the audience's interest quickly and fade away.

And of course new genres continue to emerge. For example, blockbuster franchises like the seventeen (to date) movies from the so-called Marvel Cinematic Universe, and the five (and counting) entries from Warner's "DC Cinematic Universe" are all superhero movies, a rapidly emerging genre that has grown darker and more effects-laden since the modern genre's birth in Richard Donner's *Superman* (1978). In a related vein, some movies create hybrids by combining elements of multiple genres, such as the blend of horror romance found in the Twilight series, or the horror comedy of movies like *Scream*, *Shaun of the Dead*, and *The Cabin in the Woods*. Hybrids like *The LEGO Movie* and Quentin Tarantino's *Kill Bill* films so ingeniously merge multiple references and traits that they transcend any easy genre categorization.

When studying any genre film, be sensitive to its ratio of inventiveness to conventionality, its expression of genre elements, the ways that it reflects its historical and cultural moment, and the degree to which it self-consciously asserts its status *as* genre. These questions can help you get started in your analysis:

Does the film you're analyzing seem to fit into a particular genre? In what way(s)?

Does the film fulfill your expectations about that genre, or does it seem to work against some of the traditional conventions of the genre? Again, in what way(s)?

Which conventions of the genre does the movie place greatest emphasis on? Themes? Character types? Setting? Iconographic imagery? Casting of actors well known in the genre?

Which conventions of the genre does the movie underplay or ignore?

In viewing two films from the same genre made at different times, what differences do you see? What do those differences suggest to you about the evolution of the genre during the years between the two films?

If the film doesn't seem to fit into an identifiable genre, does it nonetheless borrow or blend elements from other genres? If so, how does it use those elements? What is the purpose of this borrowing and blending?

Historical Analysis

In just over 100 years, the cinema, like the classical art forms that preceded it—architecture, fiction, poetry, drama, dance, painting, and music—has developed its own aesthetics, conventions, influence, and, of course, history. Broadly defined, film history traces the development of moving images from early experiments with photography, through the invention of the movies in the early 1890s, to the subsequent stylistic, financial, technological, and social developments in cinema that have occurred up to now.

To get some idea of the scope and depth of that record, you might browse through a comprehensive history of film, such as the ten-volume History of American Cinema series (University of California Press). Such comprehensive histories take many years, and often the efforts of many people, to get written. Because of this, most film historians don't undertake such massive projects. Most people who practice film history instead focus their energies on studying specific moments, movements, and phenomena. Jeanine Basinger's *The Star Machine* (New York: Knopf, 2007), for example, provides a masterly account of the Hollywood studio system during a very specific era (the so-called "golden age") and how it created its stars. C. S. Tashiro's *Pretty Pictures: Production Design and the History of Film* (Austin: University of Texas Press, 1998) limits its scope to focus on one aspect of film production—production design—even as it ranges widely over the full chronology of film history. In these studies and others like them, the film historian is interested equally in change—those developments that have altered the course of film history—and stability—those aspects that have defied change.

Like other historians, film historians use artifacts to study the past. These artifacts include the various machines and other technology—the cameras, projectors, sound-recording devices, etc.—without which there would be no movies. They might also include notes from story conferences, screenplays, production logs, drawings, outtakes, and other objects relevant to the production of a particular movie. Obviously, the most important artifacts to the film historian are the movies themselves.

Film history includes the history of technologies, the people and industrial organizations that produce the movies, the national cinemas that distinguish one country's movies from another's, the attempts to suppress and censor the movies, and the meanings and pleasure that we derive from watching a good film. Gaining knowledge about these and other aspects of film history is pleasurable and interesting in and of itself. But as you graduate from merely watching movies to looking at movies in a critically aware way, your knowledge of film history will also provide you with the perspective and context to understand and evaluate the unique attributes of movies, both past and present.

BASIC APPROACHES TO FILM HISTORY

Although there are many approaches to studying film history (including studies of production, regulation, and reception), the beginner should know the four traditional approaches: aesthetic, technological, economic, and social. In what follows, we describe each approach and cite one or two studies as exemplary models of each.

The aesthetic approach

Sometimes called the *masterpiece approach* or *great man approach*, this approach seeks to evaluate individual movies and/or directors using criteria that assess their artistic significance and influence. Ordinarily, historians who take this approach will first define their criteria of artistic excellence and then ask the following questions: What are the significant works of the cinematic art? Who are the significant directors? Why are these movies and these directors important? Historians who take the aesthetic perspective do not necessarily ignore the economic, technological, and cultural aspects of film history—indeed, it would be impossible to discuss many great movies without considering these factors—but they are primarily interested in movies that are not only works of art, but are also widely acknowledged masterpieces. The most comprehensive, one-volume international history that takes an aesthetic approach is David A. Cook's *A History of Narrative Film* (New York: Norton, 2015).

Auteurism. Within the category of the aesthetic approach is an approach called *auteurism*. The auteur theory postulates the film director as the *auteur* (author) of a film. Its application usually takes one of two forms: a judgment of the whole body of a film director's work based on style, or a classification of directors based on directorial styles. Auteurist criticism can be a useful exercise when one is trying to understand, for example, what makes a film a "Hitchcock" (or for that matter, a "Tarantino") film. A director must have made a significant body of films to be considered an auteur. Auteurists believe, to varying degrees, that a film director's style can (and should, according to Alexandre Astruc, one of the approach's leading advocates) be as distinctive as a novelist's. If the director is the visionary, the one person who makes a film what it is, then cinematic style is the DNA by which that "author" can be identified.

The idea of the author's presence in a cinematic work has been long debated. Whereas some critics argue that a work's coherence depends on the vision and decisions of a single person, critics in the opposing camp believe that it's the structure of a work—and not the personality that created it—that we can justly address.

Complicating the matter further is the fact that film is a collaborative medium. It's important to understand that no one person can control the product. The director of photography, the screenwriters (often many), the wardrobe and makeup people, the head of the studio—all these and others have a hand in determining the final product of a film.

Still, auteur criticism is widely practiced and is useful in helping us understand the common themes and aesthetic decisions in films by the same director (or producer, or star). Keep in mind, however, that the best of the auteur criticism draws on other sources, like film history or formal analysis, to ensure that the critique is not simply an examination of the private life or the psychology of the auteur. A fine example of the auteurist approach is James Naremore's *On Kubrick* (London: BFI, 2007).

The technological approach

All art forms have a technological history that records the advancements in materials and techniques that have affected the nature of the medium. Of all the arts, though, cinema seems to rely most heavily on technology. Historians who chart the history of cinema technology examine the circumstances surrounding the development of each technological advance, as well as subsequent improvements. They pose questions such as: When was each invention made? Under what circumstances—including aesthetic, economic, and social—was it made? Was it a totally new idea or one linked to the existing state of technology? What were the consequences for directors, studios, distributors, exhibitors, and audiences? By studying major developments (including the introduction of sound, the moving camera, color film stock, and digital cinematography), historians show us how the production of movies has changed. They can also evaluate whether or not that change was significant (like widescreen processes) or transitory (like Smell-O-Vision).

An excellent example of a study that explores technological history in conjunction with other aspects of film history is David Bordwell, Janet Staiger, and Kristin Thompson's *The Classical Hollywood Cinema: Film Study and Mode of Production to 1960* (New York: Columbia University Press, 1985). A wonderful example of a study of a specific technological subject is John Belton's *Widescreen Cinema* (Cambridge, Mass.: Harvard University Press, 1992).

The economic approach

The motion-picture industry is a major part of the global economy. Every movie released has an economic history of its own, as well as a place in the economic history of its studio and the historical period and country in which it was produced. Historians interested in this subject help us to understand how and why the studio system was founded, how it adapted to changing conditions (economic, technological, social, and historical), why different studios took different approaches to producing different movies, how these movies have been distributed and exhibited, and what effect this particular economic history had on film history. Scholars who take an economic approach study how the independent system of production superseded the studio system, and what effect this has had on production, distribution, and exhibition. They are also concerned with such related issues as management and organization, accounting and marketing practices, and censorship and the rating system. Excellent examples of such studies include Douglas Gomery's *The Hollywood Studio System: A History* (London: BFI, 2005), Joel W. Finler's *The Hollywood Story*, 3rd ed. (London: Wallflower, 2003), and Tino Balio's *Grand Design: Hollywood as a Modern Business Enterprise, 1930–1939*, History of the American Cinema series, vol. 5 (Berkeley: University of California Press, 1995).

Film as social history

Because society and culture influence the movies, and vice versa, the movies are good sources for studying society. Writing about movies as social history continues to be a major preoccupation of journalists, scholars, and students alike. Historian Ian Jarvie suggests that, in undertaking these studies, we ask the following basic questions: Who made the movies, and why? Who saw the films, how, and why? What was seen, how, and why? How were the movies evaluated, by whom, and why? In addition, those interested in social history consider such factors as religion, politics, cultural trends, and taboos, asking to what extent a particular movie was produced to sway public opinion or effect social change.

These social historians are also interested in audience composition, marketing, and criticism as it appeared in all media, from gossip magazines to scholarly books. Overall, they study the complex interaction between film as a social institution and other social institutions, including government, religion, and labor. Landmark studies include Robert Sklar's *Movie-Made America: A Cultural History of American Movies*, rev. and updated ed. (New York: Vintage, 1994), and Richard Abel's *Americanizing the Movies and "Movie-Mad" Audiences, 1910–1914* (Berkeley: University of California Press, 2006).

Here are some ways that you can make your film analyses—regardless of their primary topic or approach—more historically aware:

As you study a particular film (or film artist, style, or movement), learn as much as you can about its historical context: the year in which it was made/released; the country of origin; why, if relevant, that year was important to that country's history; how, if relevant, the movie deals with the events of that period; the means of production (e.g., studio, independent, government-sponsored); the audience for which it was intended; its reception by the public and critics alike. Isolate and identify the movie as closely as you can within this overall context.

Also learn about the film's aesthetic context: Was it made as part of a particular film movement (e.g., Italian neorealism), or does it break from the prevailing tradition of the period? If it is representative of a movement, how does it measure up against the movement's ideals and achievements? Is it part of a "national cinema" with its own aesthetic, political, and cultural values?

Learn something about its director's overall body of work. Is he regarded as an auteur? If so, how is this movie similar to, or different from, his other films? Since you may not have time to see many of the director's movies, you might compare the director's most famous movie with the one you are analyzing.

Similarly, you may want to study the history of a creative artist in the historical context of a particular genre. A few suggestions are Hayao Miyazaki's anime style within the history of animation, Preston Sturges's screenplays for 1930s screwball comedies, Freddie Young's cinematography for the historical epics directed by David Lean, Ann Roth's approach to designing costumes for period movies, Walter Murch's sound designs for the movies of Francis Ford Coppola, or the production design of films about the Civil War, from D. W. Griffith's *The Birth of a Nation* (1915) to Anthony Minghella's *Cold Mountain* (2003).

When movies have been inspired by a historical period or event (e.g., the Great Depression, the Vietnam War, the rise and fall of Rome), you have a rich opportunity to analyze and understand those cinematic interpretations. First, you should understand the complexity of this historical event by taking notes on how different historians have treated it—in other words, you should work to understand that all historical accounts are themselves interpretations of events. Your notes will help you to establish a context for determining the scope, thoroughness, and effectiveness of the movies inspired by the event.

Have you found that a particular movie has made important innovations in cinematic language or in the use of technology? If so, what are they? Who was principally responsible for these innovations (e.g., the director, sound designer, cinematographer)? Was this a momentary blip on film history's screen, or did it become a permanent part of cinematic technique or language?

If the movie you are analyzing was the product of a particular Hollywood studio, find out if that studio had a unified style for most of its movies or if it encouraged its directors to use different styles. If the former, how well does the movie evoke that style? If the latter, how does the movie's style differ? And did this film influence subsequent studio productions?

- The "reception" of a film can be as interesting as its form. Some movies, such as *Gone With the Wind* (1939), were instant successes, as popular with audiences at the time as they have proven to be over the years since first release. Others, such as *Night of the Hunter* (1955), languished in theaters during their initial release but became more highly regarded and more popular as time passed. Whatever movie you analyze, take some time to familiarize yourself with its reception history. Consider the early reviews and audience responses, the box-office receipts, the "buzz" that accompanied the release (or didn't), and the longer-term critical and popular opinion about the film.

Nearly any film essay can make use of historical facts and references. Keeping a historical perspective in the back of your mind can inform your writing even if the assignment calls primarily for a formal analysis. The typical film paper is a vehicle for exploring and explicating film form, perhaps with some use of theory, or perhaps with an eye to exploring cultural issues through films. But film history—if your instructor encourages you to pursue it—is a rich source of information that can transform a film paper into a work of considerable interest and achievement.

Now that we've looked at the wide-ranging field of film study and discussed the various tools and concerns that film scholars bring to their own writing, let's look at the *process* of writing academic papers in film courses. The following chapters will offer you good advice that you can use not only in your film courses, but in many of your other courses as well. As you read about and practice the following strategies, pay attention to which work best for you, and which might become strategies that you can use more broadly in all of your writing.

Part II

THE WRITING PROCESS

5

Generating Ideas

In some ways writing about film is similar to writing on any subject: you must choose a topic, generate ideas, research your topic, craft a thesis, structure your argument, and find the proper tone. But each of these more general tasks requires you to perform some tasks that are specific to the study of film. For instance, you must look at movies with a more critical and analytical eye (which the preceding three chapters are intended to help you do), you must be able to use specialized language appropriately, and you must know how to use research resources effectively. The following section combines general advice with suggestions specific to film studies, with the aim of helping you to produce better papers for your film class.

Generating Ideas

While viewing the movie you've chosen or that was assigned to you, you will usually come up with some ideas worth writing about. But what if you've watched the film a few times and you still haven't found anything that you feel is worth exploring? Or what if you've found an idea for writing, but you haven't yet discovered how you might develop that idea? In any of these situations you might want to take the time to try one of the following strategies for generating ideas.

CONVERSATION

After seeing a movie, we typically talk about it with others as soon as we leave the venue. Those conversations often leave us thinking about the movie in new and interesting ways. Note, however, that the kinds of conversations that we have with our friends—which are often freewheeling, opinionated, and more emotional than intellectual—mark just the beginning of scholarly inquiry. Still, talking with friends can be useful in exploring differences of opinion and in encouraging you to articulate and back up your point of view.

BRAINSTORMING

Another way to formulate ideas is to brainstorm. Brainstorming is useful because it is a quick and efficient way of laying out what you know about a subject. By brainstorming, you might also see what you don't know about a topic, which might move you to read and think further.

Suppose you decided to brainstorm for a paper on the film *Brokeback Mountain* (2005; director Ang Lee). You might make a list like the one we offer here:

Brokeback Mountain

- Is controversial in its subject matter
- Is beautifully shot
- Has a lonely feeling
- Is in some ways pretty conventional
- Has the sweeping panoramas of the western
- Has minimal dialogue, typical of the western
- Has the plot structure of a doomed love story
- Portrays the women as helpless
- Won the Academy Award for directing but not for best picture

As this list illustrates, *brainstorming* is an informal strategy for invention in which you jot down, as quickly as you can, ideas concerning your topic. The ideas don't have to be connected—though sometimes looking for connections will yield a paper topic. For instance, you might want to write a paper arguing that *Brokeback* is a more conventional film than most people think. Or you might want to write about how the spaces and silences of the film contribute to conveying the characters' essential loneliness.

Remember that you can also stop at any point in the writing process to brainstorm, especially when you feel that you're stuck or that you have to fill in some gaps in your argument. In short, when you brainstorm you freely explore your topic without the pressure of structure, grammar, or style. In the process, ideas for an essay (or a paragraph, or even a footnote) evolve unhindered.

FREEWRITING

Freewriting is similar to brainstorming in that it is a quick and informal way to develop an idea. But whereas brainstorming most often involves making a list of ideas, freewriting requires that you try to elaborate on these ideas by writing about them, without paying close attention to syntax or grammar. In this way, freewriting can get you "unstuck" when coming up with ideas is difficult.

Here's an example (and note that this freewriting, since it is meant for the writer's eyes only, is very informal—with spelling, grammar, and punctuation errors intact):

> OK, so i just saw apocalypse now and, wow, i'm supposed to write a paper on it but i have no idea what i'm going to say. the film hit me in a place where language doesn't live but still i gotta come up with something. where to start? maybe i should begin at the beginning, because from the first scene coppola grabs you and pulls you in, not just into vietnam but also into the mind of the protagonist, willard. I mean from the start you know that it's all insane—willard's insane and so is vietnam and somehow the two

insanities are the same, one is causing the other in a crazy vicious cycle. how does coppola do this? hmmmm. i guess that a lot of it has to do with the sound mix. first of all there's the great song by the doors—"the end"—which is apocalyptic and reminds us how crazy the sixties were. And willard is in this hotel room and this song is going on and we see willard sweating in this hot hotel room in Hanoi, losing his mind, and then we hear the ceiling fan that swoops menacingly overhead. And the fan blurs with the sounds of helicopters and the other sounds of the war. And you feel like the sounds outside and the sounds inside are all blending into each other. And then at the height of the insanity willard tears up the hotel room, breaks a mirror, bleeds on the sheets, and lets out a howl, which you don't hear. that's cool. you watch willard fall apart but you don't hear him screaming. you hear all the other stuff but you don't hear the scream. i wonder why coppola decided to do it this way? maybe i could think more about the sound editing in that first scene, maybe do a paper on that and how coppola manages to use sound to show the inner and outer insanities? hmmmm. i guess this was a pretty successful freewrite. all i had to do was push buttons and some ideas popped out. pushing buttons is a lot more fun than just sitting and staring at a blank screen.

DISCOVERY DRAFT

A discovery draft is another strategy for coming up with or developing your ideas. A discovery draft is similar to freewriting in that you can write freely, with little thought to the structure and the development of your ideas for the time being. You can also forget about matters of syntax and style. However, writing a discovery draft is different from freewriting in that a discovery draft makes a conscious attempt to focus on and develop an idea or a cluster of ideas. In other words, a discovery draft is like freewriting with an agenda. And because you have an agenda, a discovery draft tends to be more structured than freewriting, and to be written more or less coherently, in complete sentences.

Think of writing a discovery draft as writing a letter to an imaginary friend about your paper. Suppose that you've just seen *Memento* (2001). You might first summarize, for your friend's benefit, the film and the issues it presents. You might then raise questions about the film. You might challenge the filmmaker on certain points. You might note continuity problems or contradictions. You might point out a certain part of the film that you found compelling. You might address and then work out any confusion that you have about the topic. In writing the discovery draft you might have an aha! moment, in which you see something you hadn't seen before, and break off mid-sentence to explore it.

In a sense, the aha! moment is the point of the discovery draft. When writing the discovery draft, your thoughts are focused on your topic. You're giving language to your questions and observations. In this process, the mind almost always stumbles across something new—makes a *discovery*. And with this discovery, a paper is often launched.

Creating a discovery draft is more formal than a freewriting exercise. It always uses complete sentences and correct grammar, and it follows a logical train of thought. However, it's still not nearly as formal as a paper that you would hand in to your professor. It uses casual, colloquial language, and it doesn't state ideas as strongly as it might (because as you write a discovery draft, you're often still trying to figure out what exactly those ideas are). It also typically uses some of the thoughts that showed up in the freewrite. Freewriting helps you find ideas that might be useful in your paper; the discovery draft helps you figure out how they're useful and what you might say about them. A student who takes the time to do a freewriting exercise and to compose a discovery draft will be well on the way to a solid, working thesis.

FIVE *W*s AND AN *H*

Journalism has provided us with perhaps the simplest and most familiar way of coming up with a topic: simply ask questions such as *who*, *what*, *when*, *where*, *why*, and *how*. Answering these questions initially doesn't seem very hard—at least until one gets to the *why* and *how*. Then it gets tricky.

Let's use this method to try to generate ideas, once again, for a paper on Francis Ford Coppola's *Apocalypse Now* (1979).

Maybe when you were watching *Apocalypse Now* you got interested in Coppola's use of voice-over, so you have a topic you want to explore. Now begin your interrogation:

Where in the film does Coppola use voice-over? (Mark the scenes.)

Who is speaking during the voice-over?

What was happening in those moments? (Summarize the action.)

How is the voice-over used? (Analyze. Is Coppola using the voice-over to restore order when the narrative slips into chaos?)

When does the voice-over work best? (Evaluate its effectiveness. Is order really restored?)

Why does the film end without a final voice-over comment? Why does it end in silence?

These are tough questions. But it's precisely when you have difficulty answering a *why* question that a real paper is beginning. When the answer comes too easily, you're on familiar ground, so you're probably not saying anything interesting. Cultivate a taste for confusion. Then cultivate a strategy for clearing up confusion. Only when you ask a question that initially confuses you can real thinking and real writing begin.

TAGMEMICS

Tagmemics is a system that allows you to look at a single object from three different perspectives. One of these perspectives (or even all three) can help you determine a subject for writing. By extending an analogy regarding the different ways that physicists think about light, tagmemics involves seeing your topic:

as a particle (as a thing in itself);
as a wave (as a thing changing over time);
as part of a field (as a thing in its context).

Suppose you want to write a paper on Merian Cooper and Ernest Schoedsack's *King Kong* (1933). If you use tagmemics as a system of invention, you will begin by looking at *King Kong* as a thing in itself. In other words, what elements of this 1933 film are worth noting?

Next you might consider how the film has changed over time. How was the film received in its day? How does this reception compare to current assessments of the film? Consider the Peter Jackson remake (2005). What elements of the film have changed in the remake? How has the approach to the King Kong story changed over time?

Finally, consider *King Kong* (1933) as a thing in context. Relate it to its culture, to its moment in time. What was happening in the world in 1933? Even unlikely events and figures may provide an interesting context. For instance, in 1933 the United States was in the middle of the Great Depression, and Hitler was named chancellor of Germany. Might these events be reflected in the film in some way? How? And why?

ARISTOTLE'S TOPOI

As one of the fathers of rhetoric, Aristotle worked to formalize a system for conceiving, organizing, and expressing ideas. We're concerned here with what Aristotle called the "topoi"—a system of specific strategies for invention. Think of the topoi as a series of questions that you might ask of a film—questions that might lead you to interesting paper topics. The topoi are especially helpful when you're asked to explore a topic that seems very broad. Consider, for instance, how using the topoi can help you to write a paper on the importance of *Star Wars* to the sci-fi genre.

Use Definition

You can use definition in two ways to come up with or develop a topic. First, you might look at *genus*, which Aristotle explains as defining a general idea within specific limits. For example, you could define the sci-fi genre with the intent of showing how *Star Wars* (1977) epitomizes the elements of that genre.

The second way to use definition is to think in terms of *division*. In other words, try to think of your subject in terms of its parts. For example, consider the elements of the Star Wars franchise that best explain its popular success.

Use Comparison

You can generate ideas by making comparisons in two ways. The first is to look for *similarities* and/or *differences*. For example, you might consider how the Star Wars franchise is similar to, or stands apart from, other science-fiction franchises.

The second method is to compare *degree*. In other words, you might consider how something is better or worse than something else. For example, is *Star Wars* (1977) more important to the genre than *The Matrix* (1999)? Is it less important to the genre than *2001: A Space Odyssey* (1968)?

Explore Relationships

Aristotle determined four ways of exploring relationships as a way of coming up with ideas for writing. The first is to consider either the *cause* of your subject or its *effects*. For example, you might research the effects that *Star Wars* (1977) had on subsequent sci-fi films.

Second, you might consider a subject's *antecedent* and *consequences*. In other words, you might ask of your subject: If this, then what? For example, if *Star Wars* hadn't been made, would science fiction movies still be stuck in the B movie genre?

Third, you might examine *contraries*, or make an argument by proving its opposite. An example is to say that war is bad in order to convey the idea that peace is good. Along these lines, you might argue that *Star Wars* deserves to be viewed as a particularly influential film, by noting how other sci-fi films fall short.

Finally, you might look for *contradictions*, *incompatible statements*, or *controversy*. For example, some critics feel that *Star Wars* deserves critical acclaim, while others feel that it's overrated. You can explore the controversy and stake a claim of your own.

Examine Circumstances

In seeking an idea for a paper, you can examine circumstances in two ways. The first is to argue what's possible by asserting what's impossible. For example, you might argue that it's impossible to find a sci-fi series that is more influential than the Star Wars franchise series.

The second strategy is to consider the past or to look to the future. For example, in what ways does *Star Wars* influence the sci-fi films being produced today? What trends do we see that might allow us to predict the direction of future sci-fi films?

Rely on Testimony

The opinions of others can be a source for your paper. Look to authorities, testimonials, statistics, maxims, laws, and precedents. For example, read what Joseph Campbell says on the mythic/heroic structure of *Star Wars*. Find other authorities and listen to what they have to say.

Developing Your Ideas

You've done some preliminary brainstorming. Perhaps you've even completed a discovery draft. The problem sitting before you now is that you have too many ideas and you don't know what to do with them, or the ideas you've come up with don't seem to be sufficiently academic. What do you try next?

NUTSHELLING

Nutshelling is the simple process of trying to explain the main point of your observations in a few sentences—in a nutshell. When you put your thoughts in a nutshell, you come to see just how those thoughts fit together. You see how each thought is relevant to the others, and what the overall point is. In short, nutshelling helps you to transform your observations or information into something meaningful, focused, and coherent.

Imagine, for example, that you're asked in an assignment to consider whether or not, from your point of view, Philip Seymour Hoffman deserved to win the Best Actor Oscar for his portrayal of Truman Capote in the film *Capote* (2005). You actually have a lot to say about this. First, although Hoffman's performance was superb (in fact, you loved it), you think that Heath Ledger's portrayal of a gay cowboy in *Brokeback Mountain* was more Oscar-worthy. Why? Well, when you were watching *Brokeback*, you forgot you were watching Heath Ledger play a gay cowboy; when you were watching *Capote*, you were always aware that you were watching Hoffman taking on Capote's skin. In your opinion, making the audience forget that they're watching a celebrity is harder than imitating (however brilliantly) another celebrity. But you're pretty sure the academy doesn't agree with you. After all, they gave the Oscar to Nicole Kidman for playing Virginia Woolf, and to Jamie Foxx for playing Ray Charles.

In a nutshell, what is your take on the matter? After considering all of your feelings on the subject, you decide that, although Philip Seymour Hoffman's performance was Oscar-worthy, his win over Heath Ledger reveals how celebrity-obsessed the voting members of the academy are. Stated more fully,

> When actors in biopics meet the challenges of re-creating a character, they dazzle us: it seems as if they've managed to resurrect their subjects before our very eyes. And yet this resurrection shouldn't be the determining criterion for awarding the Oscar, as it has been in the last few years. Philip Seymour Hoffman's win over Heath Ledger in the 2006 Oscar race illustrates the tendency of Oscar voters to reward celebrities playing other celebrities, indicating the Academy's own obsession with celebrity culture.

In the process of nutshelling you've done more than come up with a promising idea for a paper; you've also come up with a promising plan for your entire introduction. Nutshelling has proven to be a successful prewriting strategy in this case.

BROADENING YOUR TOPIC

What happens when you've put your thoughts in a nutshell and they seem too "small"? You may have come up with a topic that's too narrow, too particular to support a sustained conversation.

Say, for example, that you've been asked to watch a film and to observe the makeup and costuming. You've noticed that the filmmaker seems to focus on women and lipstick. The film has a key scene of women discussing their sex lives as they try on lipstick at a cosmetics counter. Throughout the film, the director makes sure that we notice lipstick by offering lingering close-ups of women putting on lipstick, of lipstick stains on glasses, and so on.

You've made notes about these lipstick scenes, and you think that you can write an essay that chronicles the use of lipstick as a metaphor in this film. But it's not enough simply to chronicle the appearance of lipstick in the film. Instead, you have to talk about *how* the director uses these images and then make a declaration about what this recurring image *means*.

After writing your discovery draft, you come up with the idea that the filmmaker uses lipstick to call attention to the fact that the characters are trying to mask their feelings. Though this observation is a promising one, it still isn't "big" enough. Why not? Because it remains an observation, not an argument; it lists *how* A, B, and C mask their feelings without addressing the matter of *why* this masking is important to consider. How do you broaden your topic so that you feel you have something important to say?

First, try to make connections. Do the characters rely on other ways of masking themselves? Is masking one of the film's central themes? In what other ways does the director explore the idea of masking?

Second, turn your idea inside out. Consider the other side of the matter. For example, lipstick might be part of a character's mask, but it also calls attention to that character. Lipstick doesn't give her a mask to hide behind; instead it screams, "Hey! Look at me!" This is interesting. Perhaps the character exaggerates certain qualities in order to hide others. Is this sleight of hand (reveal/conceal) at work elsewhere in the film?

Third, consider the context. There are, of course, at least two contexts to consider: the context *within* the film, and the context *without*. With*in* the film, you might seek a context for lipstick. What's happening, exactly, when the characters put on lipstick? Is this act presented by the filmmaker as being positive or negative? What values does the film assert, and how does the use of lipstick reflect or challenge these values? What is the film's theme, and how does lipstick reflect or challenge that?

With*out* the film are other contexts. Consider, for instance, the filmmaker's other works. Is masking an important issue there? Consider some of the cultural forces at work. What larger social issue might the filmmaker be highlighting? Finally, masking is an ancient practice. What can you find out about the history of masking that is relevant to the matter at hand?

All of these questions might help you broaden your topic so that your discussion is substantial and interesting.

NARROWING/FOCUSING YOUR TOPIC

What if your topic seems too big to handle? What do you do then?

Let's consider the hypothetical film that we were just discussing.

Perhaps, after doing the various prewriting exercises, you've concluded that all the characters in this film seem to wear masks. Although this observation is potentially fruitful, you should resist the temptation to be satisfied with it. After all, a paper showing that Mary wears a mask and Johnny wears a mask and Caroline wears a mask will probably bore the reader. It will seem like a string of obvious and general observations. How do you focus your topic?

First, test your claim. A statement as broad as this one is probably not always true. Do all the characters wear masks, or just some of them? You might discover that only the female characters wear masks. Or you might discover that, while these women wear makeup (a kind of physical mask), it's the men in the film whose feelings are most concealed. These more focused observations lead to a more interesting, more manageable topic.

Then look for examples. Remember that broad is also *vague*. Focusing on specific examples can make a topic clearer. For instance, you might want to consider when, specifically, the characters try to mask themselves. Do they mask themselves in every moment of the film, or only at those moments that are crucial to their destinies? Are they cowards, or is the filmmaker trying to say that it's right for people to try to protect themselves from the cruelty of fate?

Look for more examples. How do people mask themselves? Reconsider the lipstick idea. Perhaps the use of lipstick in the film signifies the impulse to mask.

Finally, consider the context. Just as a consideration of context can help you broaden an idea, it can also help you focus it. "Everybody masks" can therefore become "Historically, people have used masks in these particular ways. Filmmaker X uses masks in similar ways to argue Y." Then show (1) how the characters use masks in traditional ways, and (2) what the filmmaker is trying to illustrate through these allusions to the historical uses of the mask.

Essentially, you are looking for details that support your specific claim while simultaneously weeding out other parts of the film because they're not important to your argument. If you fail to go through that process, you may end up including extraneous information in your essay, and your instructor will likely tell you that the paper seems disorganized. If you do a good job of narrowing your focus, that won't be a problem.

Thinking Beyond the Frame

So far, we've been advising you to consider the formal aspects of a film's composition. As we pointed out earlier, however, you can write about film in several ways. Sometimes you will want to "think beyond the frame" and consider questions about how the film was made, its historical context, and so on. Keeping in mind what you learned in Chapter 3, ask yourself the following questions:

Who made the film? Find out who directed the film and what other films this director has made. If you've seen some of these other films, you'll have a better understanding of the themes and genres that interest the director.

What is the production history of the film? See if you can find out anything about the conditions under which the film was made. *Apocalypse Now*, for example, has an interesting production history, in terms of its financing, casting, writing, and so on. Knowing something about the film's production can help you understand some of the aesthetic and cinematic choices that the director has made.

What do the critics and scholars say? Reading what others have said about the film before you see it may help you focus your observations. If a film is particularly well known for the editing of a certain scene [the shower scene in Hitchcock's *Psycho* (1960), for example], you'll want to pay close attention to the editing when you view the film.

What can you learn from the film's genre? Before you see the film, think a bit about the norms and limitations of its genre. When you view the film, you can then consider how these limitations are enforced or challenged. For example, Clint Eastwood's *Unforgiven* (1992) is a western that challenges its genre's typical notions of good guy versus bad guy. Knowing how this dynamic plays itself out in other westerns helps you understand and appreciate Eastwood's accomplishment.

Does the work reflect an interesting cultural phenomenon? Sometimes a professor will ask you to watch certain films because he wants you to examine a cultural phenomenon—for example, the phenomenon of stardom. Accordingly, you might watch Roland Joffé's *The Scarlet Letter* (1995) with the idea of viewing it as a "star vehicle," contributing to Demi Moore's star persona. Note that this sort of paper may also be a discussion of formal analysis; for example, you might discuss how Demi Moore was lit in certain scenes to emphasize her position as Hollywood star.

If asking these questions leads you to a promising topic, but you find that you don't know enough to write about the topic without reading other sources, then you will need to conduct research in order to write your paper. The next chapter provides some guidance on the research process.

6

Researching Movies

Doing research in a film class is in many ways similar to doing research for other classes: you'll visit the library or the library's databases, find books and journals, get a clear sense of the scholarly conversation, and then offer a perspective of your own. One important difference, though, is that when you write about movies the film itself is typically the primary source, with film criticism (books, journal articles, and so on) serving as secondary sources.

Understanding Primary and Secondary Sources

Primary sources are defined as any text, object, photograph, film, or other medium that is the object of scholarly investigation. A *secondary source*, on the other hand, is a work that analyzes, comments on, or otherwise sheds light on the primary text, historical event, object, or phenomenon in question.

A source can be primary or secondary, depending on the purpose of your research. For instance, you might write a film paper in which the primary text is something other than a movie (e.g., a filmmaker's journal, shooting script, or shot list). Or you might write a paper in which a secondary source consists of film footage (e.g., an "extra" feature on a DVD).

As we continue this discussion about research, we'll be talking in most cases about secondary sources that comment on film (e.g., film history, film criticism, and theoretical articles).

Using Sources

Having a strategy for collecting and employing sources is a good idea. No one wants to wander from source to source trying to remember what, precisely, that source argued, or why it mattered in the first place. We therefore offer the following research tips, which we think will help you become a more effective and efficient researcher.

It may seem at first that these steps take time. "Why should I stop to summarize a source when I can simply go back to the original?" you might wonder. However, the strategies outlined here will save you time in the long run. The work you do to digest and classify your sources as you do your research will make the writing process much more focused, much more efficient, and much less painful in the end.

SUMMARIZE YOUR SOURCES

Before attempting to use any source in your paper, make sure you understand it. The best way to do this is to summarize the source. In summarizing, you accomplish a few things. First, summarizing a source requires you to put the argument in your own language. Some of your secondary sources might use language that puzzles you. When you summarize, you are, in a sense, translating an argument into language that you understand and can work with. Summarizing also helps you see whether there's any aspect of the argument that you aren't getting. If you find yourself stumbling as you attempt to summarize, go back to the original source for clarity.

Summarizing also allows you to restate an argument in terms that are relevant to your paper. Most film criticism that you will encounter is very complex and offers several ideas for consideration. Some of these ideas will be relevant to your topic, while others will not. When you summarize, you can restate the part of the argument that seems most relevant to the paper you want to write.

Summarizing can also help you organize your source material. If you've used ten sources in a research project, you've probably taken a lot of notes and gathered several quotations for your paper. This work can amount to pages and pages of text. Summaries can help you organize these notes by telling you almost at a glance which idea comes from which source. You can also include in your summaries a few of the best quotations from each source.

Finally, summarizing is helpful to the entire research process. It's not something that you should do once at the beginning of the research process and then forget about. Every time your understanding of the topic shifts or evolves, take the time to write a brief summary. You'll find that putting your thoughts into writing helps you solidify one stage of understanding before progressing to the next.

CATEGORIZE YOUR SOURCES

Once you've summarized your sources, try to place them into various categories. Remember, writing an academic essay is like taking part in a large, ongoing conversation. Although everyone has a particular point of view, it's safe to say that no one is entering the conversation as a lone wolf. Everyone is speaking from a certain critical perspective. These perspectives might be classified into different groups.

Categorizing your sources might be as simple as looking for similarities among them. Which sources seem to share a point of view? Which seem to arrive at similar conclusions? You will also discover differences among your sources. Try to define these differences and see if they seem to fall into different categories. For example, side A seems to believe X, while side B seems to believe Y. Or, side A attempts to understand the literary work from a feminist perspective, while side B is interested in interpreting the work from a socioeconomic perspective.

Once you've categorized your sources, try to understand what these differences and similarities mean to your argument. Are these categories relevant to the issues you intend to discuss? Where does your own argument fit in? Does the reader need to know about these categories for your argument to make sense? Try to articulate these matters clearly. Write a summary of what you think at this point.

INTERROGATE YOUR SOURCES

In most of the papers that you'll write in college, you'll have to do more than review what other people have said about a topic. You will be asked to present your own point of view. To do this, you'll need to interrogate your sources.

Interrogating your sources does not mean that you have to be contentious. You don't have to search like a bloodhound for the weak spot in an argument. You're not required to "take on" your source. Instead, you'll want to ask questions of your sources. Initiate a conversation. Challenge, interrogate, rebut, and confirm. Some good questions to ask are the following:

Is the writer offering evidence for her claims? Is this evidence sufficient? Why or why not?

Is there something that the writer is overlooking? Omitting? If so, is the omission a matter of carelessness, or does it seem purposeful? Why?

Does the writer's argument seem reasonable? If not, can you locate places where the reasoning seems to break down? Can you locate and identify any logical fallacies?

Is the writer's language appropriate? Does she sometimes rely on a pretty phrase or a passionate claim to cover up a lack of evidence?

What can you determine about the writer's perspective? Does she seem to have any important biases? Does she seem to belong to a particular critical school of thought? Does the writer's perspective help or hinder the argument that she's trying to make? Why?

Where do you stand in relation to the writer? Do you give her a round of applause? Do you feel like booing her off the stage? Are you sitting with your brow furrowed, feeling skeptical? Keep notes regarding your personal responses to the source, and try to translate those responses into comments or questions.

ANNOTATE YOUR SOURCES

Most scholars find it useful whenever possible to mark their texts as they read them—not simply by highlighting important passages, but by making a note of their questions and reactions in the margins. Marking your text enables you to enter into conversations with the author. No longer are you reading passively. Instead, you are reading actively, filling the margins with comments and questions that could blossom into a paper topic down the road. Annotating your texts also ensures that your questions and inspirations won't get lost. Entire books and dissertations have evolved from notes made in the margins. The ideas for these books and dissertations might have been lost had the writer not taken the time to write them down.

MAKE YOUR SOURCES WORK FOR YOU

Students often make a grave mistake when they write their first academic papers: overwhelmed by what their sources have to say, they permit their papers to crumble under the weight of scholarly opinion. They end up not writing an informed argument of their own but rehashing what has already been said on a topic. Such a paper might be informative. It might also be competently written. But it does not fulfill the requirements of a good academic paper.

Remember, a good academic paper must be analytical, it must be critical, and it must present a well-crafted, persuasive, informed argument.

Consider the phrase "informed argument." The word with the power in this phrase is the noun "argument." The word "informed" is merely a descriptor. It serves the noun, qualifying it, coloring it. The information that you gather should serve your argument in much the same way. Make your sources work for *you*.

You can take some steps to ensure that your sources do indeed work for you without overwhelming your argument. First, don't go to the library or go online before you've thought about your topic on your own. Certainly your research will have an impact on what you think. Sometimes you might even find that you reverse your opinion. But if you go to the library before you've given your topic some thought, you risk jumping on the bandwagon of the first persuasive argument you encounter.

Second, limit your sources to those that are relevant to your topic. It's easy to be swept up in the broader scholarly conversation about your subject and to go off on tangents that don't, in the end, serve your argument.

Finally, keep track of your evolving understanding of the topic by periodically stopping to summarize. As we said earlier, summarizing your sources makes them more manageable. If you manage your sources as you go along, you will reduce the risk that they'll overwhelm you later.

Keeping Track of Your Sources

During the research process it's very important to keep track of your sources. Nothing is more frustrating than having a great quotation and not knowing where it came from. Develop a good, consistent system for keeping notes.

Every academic discipline requires that you submit with your paper a bibliography or list of works cited. A bibliography should include every work you looked at in your research, even if you didn't quote that source directly. A list of works cited, on the other hand, is just that: a list of works that you quoted, paraphrased, or alluded to in the text of your paper. Both bibliographies and lists of works cited require you to provide information that will make it easier for your reader to find these sources for herself. Consult the Modern Language Association's *MLA Handbook* for information about how to construct a proper bibliography and/or list of works cited.

Citing Sources

When you write an academic paper, you must cite all the sources that you've used, even if you don't quote them directly. If you fail to cite these sources, you will be charged with plagiarism. Plagiarism (passing off as your own the words and ideas of others, whether an entire article or just one phrase) is an academic offense for which there are serious consequences.

We can offer several good reasons not to plagiarize. First, it's very easy to get caught. Your instructors—who have spent years teaching students to write and so have read countless student essays—are keenly aware of the difference between professional and student writing. They notice when sophisticated, highly polished academic writing appears out of the blue, with seemingly no development or context. In addition, although technology makes plagiarism easy, it also empowers teachers, who can use sophisticated search programs to scan literally millions of documents for suspect phrases and sentences.

Second, plagiarism cheats both the reader and the writer. At a fundamental level, citing a source is an academic courtesy. Because scholarship is an ongoing conversation, you should always presume that other students or scholars could want to use your work to develop their own. If you've taken an idea from another scholar but haven't cited it (or have cited it improperly), your reader will have no easy way of finding the source of the ideas that have found their way into your work.

Perhaps the most serious problem raised when you plagiarize or fail to cite your sources is that you're cheating yourself. When you rely on the ideas of others to meet a course requirement, you're denying yourself the opportunity to have the best experience that college can offer—the opportunity to think for yourself. Writing papers can be difficult, and when deadlines loom it can be tempting to look for a shortcut and to lift ideas from scholars who clearly know more about your topic than you do. But it's *your* perspective that your instructor wants to hear. Take each writing assignment as an opportunity to explore and express your ideas. You're paying a lot for this education; you might as well get your money's worth.

7

Developing Your Thesis

Writing a Thesis Sentence

No sentence in your paper will vex you as much as the thesis sentence, and with good reason: the thesis sentence is very often the one sentence in the paper that asserts, controls, and structures the entire argument. Without a strong, persuasive, thoughtful thesis—explicit or implied—a paper might seem unfocused, weak, and not worth the reader's time.

What makes a good thesis sentence? A good thesis sentence generally has the following characteristics:

A good thesis sentence makes a claim. This doesn't mean that you have to reduce an idea to an either/or proposition and then take a stand. Rather, you need to develop an interesting perspective that you can support and defend. This perspective must be more than an observation. "The United

States of America has a violent-crime rate more than twice that of Canada" is merely an observation (verifiable by statistical records). "Americans are more violent than Canadians because they are fearful of each other" (the position that the documentary filmmaker Michael Moore makes in *Bowling for Columbine* [2002]) is an argument. Why? Because it posits a perspective. It also makes a claim that engages competing claims. Put another way, a good thesis sentence inspires (rather than silences) other points of view. Someone else might argue that America is violent because of the disintegration of the traditional nuclear family. Another person might point to the prevalence of guns in this country. In short, if your thesis is positing something that no one can (or would bother to) argue with, then it's not a very good thesis.

A good thesis sentence determines the scope of the argument. The thesis sentence determines what you're required to say in a paper. It also determines what you cannot say. Every paragraph in your paper exists to support or develop your thesis. Accordingly, if one paragraph you've written seems irrelevant to your thesis, you have three choices: get rid of that paragraph, rewrite the thesis sentence to accommodate the paragraph, or work to make the paragraph more clearly relevant. Understand that you don't have a fourth option: you can't simply include the paragraph without making clear its connection to your thesis. The thesis is like a contract between you and your reader. If you introduce ideas that the reader isn't prepared for or doesn't find relevant, you've violated that contract.

A good thesis sentence provides a structure for the argument. The thesis sentence signals to the reader not only what your argument is but how it will be presented. In other words, your thesis sentence should either directly or indirectly suggest the structure of your argument to the reader. Say, for example, that you're going to argue the following idea: "Michael Moore plays on American fearfulness by using two techniques: A and B." In this case the reader understands that you're going to cover two important points, and that these points will appear in a certain order. If you suggest a particular ordering principle and then abandon it, the reader could feel irritated and confused.

Alternatives to the Thesis Sentence

Sometimes the purpose of a piece of writing is not to make a claim but to raise questions. Other times a writer wants to leave a matter unresolved, inspiring readers to create their own positions. In these cases the thesis sentence might take other forms: the thesis question or the implied thesis.

As we've said, not every piece of writing sets out to make a claim. If your purpose as a writer is to explore, for instance, the reasons for the financial success of James Cameron's *Avatar* (2009) (a topic for which you're not prepared to make a claim), your thesis question might read "What cultural forces conspired to make *Avatar* a popular success?"

Note that this question, while provocative, does not offer a sense of the argument's structure. It permits the writer to pursue all ideas, without committing to any. Although this freedom might seem appealing, in fact you will find that the lack of a declarative thesis statement requires more work: you need to tighten your internal structure and your transitions from paragraph to paragraph so that the essay is clear and the reader can easily follow your line of inquiry.

To illustrate, let's suppose that you want to use the thesis question "What forces conspired to make *Avatar* (2009) the highest-grossing film of all time?" You might start by discussing the history of the blockbuster since Steven Spielberg's *Jaws* (1975). You might also talk about how the themes of the movie—most prominently, the concerns among young people about environmental devastation—tapped into the zeitgeist at the time of the movie's release. You might expand your discussion to look at the appeal of technological innovations in movies, especially pathbreaking special effects techniques and the visual spectacles that they make possible.

You can see that there's a lot of material to cover here—perhaps too much. If you don't know where the paper will lead or what your conclusions will be, you might find it difficult to avoid digressing. Therefore, if you're going to use a thesis question, make sure that it's a clearly articulated question and that you can structure a well-ordered investigation in response. If the paper starts to feel unwieldy, you might decide instead to use the question as the beginning of a discovery draft. Your findings in the discovery draft can then lead to a declarative thesis for the essay.

THE IMPLIED THESIS

One of the most fascinating things about a thesis sentence is that it is the most important sentence in a paper—even when it's not there.

Some of the best writers never explicitly declare a thesis. In some essays you'll find it difficult to point to a single sentence that declares the argument. Still, the essays are coherent and make a point. In these cases the writers have used an implied thesis.

Writers use an implied thesis when they want readers to come to their own conclusions about the matter at hand. However, just because the writer doesn't declare the thesis doesn't mean that she is working without one. Good writers will clearly state a thesis—either in their own mind or in their notes for the paper. They may elect not to put the thesis in the paper, but each paragraph, each sentence that they write, is controlled by the thesis all the same.

If you decide to write a paper with an implied thesis, be sure that you have a strong grasp of your argument and its structure. Also be sure that you supply adequate transitions so that the reader can follow your argument with ease.

When you begin writing, you should have a solid, well-articulated thesis. The thesis will tell your readers the purpose of your essay, and as you write, it will help guide you. However, it's also important to keep in mind that the thesis you have when you begin is not set in stone; you can still modify it. Often you'll find that, as you write, your thoughts about the issue will evolve, and you'll refine your conclusions. Sometimes it will be necessary to change your thesis to reflect those changes in your thinking. Therefore, when you begin writing, what you really have is a *working thesis*. It can change and adapt and develop as you write the paper. A working thesis doesn't necessarily become a final thesis until the paper is finished.

Turning Your Ideas into a Thesis

Now that we've looked at what you want in a thesis, let's take a moment to look at creating one based on work you've already done. Let's say you've done some brainstorming, a little freewriting, and maybe written a discovery draft, and you've come up with some interesting thoughts. After that, you spent a little time nutshelling, trying to focus your ideas. Now you just need to convert one of those focused ideas into a working thesis.

Composing a working thesis is challenging. After all, the thesis is arguably your paper's most important sentence. It cannot be crafted formulaically but must reflect the complexities of the argument that you are hoping to write. However, even though no formula exists for writing a successful thesis, we can offer some advice to get you off on the right foot.

First you'll want to determine what you want to write about. Since you've already created some ideas through brainstorming, freewriting, and other exercises, you should have some options.

From the list of observations you generated during these idea-generating exercises, you'll want to find an observation that interests you. You might choose a single observation from your list and focus on it, or you might look for an idea that ties together two or three of these observations, and focus on that. Whatever you decide, don't try to squeeze everything you've observed into a single essay. To do so would require a book—and you simply don't have time to write a book before the paper is due. Determining which idea or set of ideas you want to work with will enable you to stay focused and to do justice to your ideas in the limited time that you have.

Sometimes writers are torn between two or three very good observations. If the ideas can't be synthesized into a single idea or claim, the best strategy is to pick whichever observation looks most interesting. In other words, choose the observation you can have the most fun with. Doing so will help you stay focused: you will now know not only what you'll want to discuss, but also what you can eliminate.

You'll also notice something interesting at this point: even though you don't yet have a thesis, the observation you've chosen to write about will help dictate which type of paper you're writing. If your observation has to do with the use of sound in a film (as in the *Apocalypse Now* example above), then you'll be writing a formal analysis paper. Realizing this helps you understand not only what you're going to do but what you're not going to do: a paper about film history, or a cultural analysis, for example.

So now you have your plan: you're going to write a specific type of paper (formal analysis) about Coppola's use of sound in *Apocalypse Now*. As we noted earlier in this guide, your goal in writing a formal analysis paper is to choose an element of the film's form and examine in detail how that element contributes to the major themes, underlying message, or overall effect of the film. At this point you need to compose a question, using this goal to guide you. After some doodling you come up with this question: How does Coppola's use of sound contribute to the overall effect of *Apocalypse Now*? Give yourself the opportunity to explore that question. Brainstorm or freewrite a response. Then try to shape your response so that you can answer the question in a couple of sentences, then a single sentence. When you can answer that question in one sentence, you'll have your working thesis.

Of course if you were writing a cultural analysis paper, you'd ask yourself a different question, based on the goals of that type of paper. The same is true for a paper that explores the place of *Apocalypse Now* in film history and cultural history. The strategy is clear: instead of trying to create a thesis out of thin air, pick an element of the movie that interests you, then ask yourself a relevant question based on the goals of the type of paper you're going to write. When you answer your own question, you'll have a working thesis.

The Thesis Sentence Checklist

In the end you may have spent a good deal of time writing your working thesis and still not know if it's a good one. As we indicated earlier, a good thesis typically evolves as the writer writes. As you write, you'll want to interrogate your thesis in order to determine how well it's holding up. Some questions to ask yourself follow:

Does the thesis sentence attempt to answer or to explore a challenging intellectual question? Consider the question that you are posing. If your question doesn't challenge you, it likely won't challenge your reader either. Nor will it lead to a thesis you and your reader care about. If you find yourself bored as you write, or if you are haunted by the sense that you aren't talking about anything important, stop writing. Return to your list of observations. See if you can find some connection between the observations that might raise the intellectual stakes.

Will the point I'm making generate discussion and argument, or will it leave people asking "So what?" If your thesis doesn't generate discussion, perhaps the point you made is too obvious. Return to your list of observations. Ask of each one, "Why is this important to the study of this film, and to the study of film in general?" The answer to this question should help you refine your thesis.

Is the thesis too vague? Too general? If a thesis is too broad, it's unlikely to hold the reader's interest. It's also unlikely to give you a clear sense of direction for your paper. Try to be more specific in your focus. Take your more general idea and apply it to specific observations about the film. Perhaps in that application you'll find the focus for your paper.

Does the thesis deal directly with the topic at hand, or is it a declaration of my personal feelings? Be careful about personal opinions: as we've noted, making a claim is different from declaring an opinion. An academic paper does the former but eschews the latter.

Does the thesis indicate the direction of my argument? Does it suggest a structure for my paper? If a thesis is well constructed, it will suggest to you and to your reader where the paper is going. Look at your thesis, then look at your outline. Does your thesis reflect or suggest that outline? Can you rewrite the thesis so that the outline/structure is suggested?

Does the introductory paragraph define terms important to my thesis? Don't make your thesis do all the work. Rely on your introduction to help your thesis, especially when it comes to necessary but cumbersome tasks, such as defining terms.

If I'm writing a research paper, does my introduction place my thesis within the larger, ongoing scholarly discussion

about the topic? Consider again the dinner-party metaphor. What do the scholars at the table have to say about the topic? What do you have to say in response to their ideas? Is the relationship between your perspective and theirs clear to the reader? If not, how might it be made clear?

8

Considering Structure and Organization

Once you've figured out what you want to say, you're left with the problem of how to say it. How should you begin the paper? Should you address the opinions of other thinkers? And what should you do with that stubborn contradiction you've uncovered in your own thinking?

Writing papers in college requires you to come up with sophisticated, complex, and even creative ways of structuring your ideas. Accordingly, we can't offer simple formulas that will work for every paper, every time. We can, however, give you some things to think about that will help you as you consider how to structure your paper.

Let Your Thesis Direct You

Begin by listening to your thesis. If it's well written, it will tell you which way to go with your paper. Suppose, for example, that, in responding to the films of the early Soviet filmmakers, you have written a thesis that says this:

> The purpose of the early Soviet films was not only to support the ideology of the revolution, but to create *Homo sovieticus*, a new kind of human being.

This thesis provides the writer with several clues about how best to structure the paper, and it prepares readers for what they will encounter therein. First, the thesis promises readers that the paper will argue that Soviet filmmakers were interested in more than ideology. The paper will therefore begin by acknowledging that although the promotion of revolutionary values was important to these filmmakers, it was not their only goal. The rest of the paper will concern the (more important) creation of *Homo sovieticus*—a new sort of human being.

We say that this idea of *Homo sovieticus* is more important than ideology not necessarily because the Soviet filmmakers said so, but because the writer seems to say so in her thesis. Reread the thesis sentence. Note that the emphasis falls on the last clause: "a new kind of human being." This emphasis tells us that we will be given not simply a description of how Soviet filmmakers propagated Soviet ideology, but rather a description of how the methods of propagating this ideology were used to create a new type of human being—a Soviet person. We understand all of this because the writer took the time to make sure that the thesis was written emphatically. (For more about sentence emphasis, see Chapter 9, "Attending to style.")

Sketching Your Argument

Although your thesis will identify your paper's general direction, it will not necessarily provide you with a plan for how to organize all of your points, large and small. Here it might be helpful to diagram or sketch your argument.

In sketching your argument, the goal is to fill the page with your ideas. Begin by writing your thesis. Put it where your instincts tell you to: at the top of the page, in the center, at the bottom. Around the thesis, cluster the points you want to make. Under each of these points, note the observations you've made and the evidence you'll use. Don't get nervous when your sketch starts to look messy. Use arrows. Draw circles. Take up colored pens. Any of these methods can help you find connections between your ideas that otherwise might go unnoticed. Working from your sketch, try to see the line of reasoning that is evolving.

Sketching is an important step in the writing process because it allows you to explore visually the connections between your ideas. If you skip sketching and outline your paper too early in the process, you risk missing these connections. You might line up your points—A, B, C—without fully understanding how they are connected. Sketching your argument helps you see, for example, that points A and C overlap and need to be thought through more carefully.

Outlining Your Argument

When you've finished the sketch, you're ready to make an outline. The task of the outline is to identify the paper's best structure. By "best structure" we mean the structure that best supports the argument you intend to make.

When you're outlining a paper, you'll have many options for organization. Understand, however, that each choice you make eliminates dozens of other options. Your goal is to come up with an outline in which all your choices support your thesis.

Treat the outline as if it were a puzzle that you are putting together. In a puzzle, each piece has only one appropriate place. The same should be true of your paper. If it's easy to shift around your ideas—if several of your paragraphs could be switched around and no one would care—then you haven't yet found the best structure for your paper. Each paragraph should present a single, well-supported idea that is the logical successor to the ideas that preceded it, all of them building inexorably toward your paper's overall point—the thesis. Keep working until your outline fits your ideas like a glove.

When you think you have an outline that works, challenge it. The first outline rarely holds up to a good interrogation. When you start asking questions of your outline, you will begin to see where the plan holds and where it falls apart. Here are some questions you might ask:

Does my thesis control the direction of the outline?

Are all of my main points relevant to the thesis?

Can any of these points be moved around without changing something important about the thesis?

Does the outline seem logical?

Does the argument progress, or does it stall?

If the argument seems to take a turn midstream, does the thesis anticipate that turn?

Do I have sufficient support for each of my points?

Have I made room in the outline for other points of view about the topic?

Does this outline reflect a thorough, thoughtful argument? Have I covered the ground?

Constructing Paragraphs

Imagine that you've written the thesis. You've interrogated the outline. You know which modes of arrangement you intend to use. You've settled on a plan that you think will work. Now you have to go about the serious business of constructing paragraphs.

You were probably told in high school that paragraphs are the workhorses of a paper. Indeed they are. If a single paragraph is incoherent or weak, the entire argument might fail. It's important that you consider carefully the "job" of each paragraph. Know what you want that paragraph to do. Make sure it fulfills that purpose.

WHAT IS A PARAGRAPH?

A paragraph is generally understood as a single "unit" of a paper. What your readers expect when they encounter a new paragraph is that you're going to declare a point and then offer support for that point. If you violate this expectation—if your paragraphs wander aimlessly among three or four points, or if they declare points without offering any evidence to support them—readers will become confused or irritated by your argument. They won't want to read any further.

WHAT SHOULD A PARAGRAPH DO?

Consider this: what you look for in a partner, a reader looks for in a paragraph. Whether in business or in life, you want a partner who is supportive, focused, strong, and considerate. Similarly, a good paragraph is:

- **Supportive.** A good paragraph supports and develops the thesis. It also declares its relationship to the thesis, making its purpose in the overall argument clear.
- **Focused.** A good paragraph focuses on a single, well-articulated argument point. It doesn't muddy the argument by focusing on too many ideas, nor does it proceed to make its argument without declaring what, in fact, it is trying to argue. Rather, a good paragraph is focused and cohesive.
- **Strong.** A good paragraph isn't bloated with irrelevancies or redundancies. Nor is it underdeveloped, lacking evidence and/or analysis. Rather, a good paragraph is intellectually "muscular." It derives its intellectual muscle from its evidence and its reasoning.
- **Considerate.** A good paragraph is considerate of its relationships to other paragraphs. It both builds from the paragraph that came before, and delivers a more developed argument to the paragraph that follows. It makes sense within the text as a whole.

WRITING THE TOPIC SENTENCE OR GUIDING CLAIM

Just as every paper requires a thesis sentence to assert and control its argument, so also every paragraph requires a topic sentence to assert and control its main idea. Without a topic sentence, your paragraphs could seem jumbled or aimless.

Your reader could become confused. Because the topic sentence plays such an important role in your paragraph, it must be crafted with care. When you've written a topic sentence, ask yourself the following questions:

Does the topic sentence declare a single point of the argument? Because the reader expects that a paragraph will explore only one argument point, it's important that your topic sentence is not too ambitious. If it points to two or three ideas, perhaps you need to consider developing more paragraphs.

Does the topic sentence further the argument? Give your topic sentences the same "so what?" test that you gave your thesis sentence. If your topic sentence isn't interesting and clear in its purpose, your paragraph probably won't further the argument. Your paper could stall.

Is the topic sentence relevant to the thesis? It might seem so to you, but the relevance may not be so clear to your reader. If you find that your topic sentence is taking you into brand-new territory, stop writing and consider your options. If the new territory isn't relevant to the existing thesis, either you'll have to rewrite your thesis to accommodate this new direction, or you'll have to consider excluding this paragraph from your final paper.

Is there a clear relationship between this topic sentence and the paragraph that came before it? Make sure that you haven't left out any steps in the process of building your argument. If you take a sudden turn in your reasoning, signify that turn to the reader by using the proper transitional phrase—"on the other hand," "however," or the like.

Does the topic sentence control the paragraph? If your paragraph seems to unravel, take a second look. Perhaps the topic sentence isn't adequately controlling the paragraph and needs to be rewritten. Or maybe the paragraph is moving on to a new idea that needs to be developed in a paragraph of its own.

Where have I placed my topic sentence? Readers often look for topic sentences at or near the beginning of a paragraph. Consider this: If you are skimming something quickly, which sentence do you look to in each paragraph? Likely it's the first sentence. This doesn't mean that all of your topic sentences need to be situated at the beginning of your paragraphs. Nevertheless, if you're going to place your topic sentence elsewhere, you'll need to craft your paragraph with care. You might justify putting the topic sentence in the middle of the paragraph, for example, if you have information that needs to precede it. You might also justify putting the topic sentence at the end of the paragraph if you want the reader to consider your line of reasoning before you declare your main point. Let the argument and what it needs dictate where you place your topic sentence. Wherever you place it, be strategic. Make sure that your decision facilitates your argument.

Developing Your Paragraphs

EVIDENCE

Students often ask how long a paragraph should be. To this we respond "As long as it takes."

It's possible to make a point quickly. Sometimes it's desirable to keep it short. Notice the preceding paragraph, for example. We might have hemmed and hawed, talked about short paragraphs and long paragraphs. We might have said that the average paragraph is one-half to two-thirds of a page in length. We might have spent time explaining why the too-short paragraph is too short, and the too-long paragraph too long. Instead, we cut to the chase. After huffing and puffing through this paragraph (which is getting longer and longer all the time), we'll give you the same advice: a good paragraph is as long as it needs to be in order to illustrate, explore, and/or prove its main idea.

However, length isn't all that matters in paragraph development. It's not even a paragraph's most important feature. What's important is that a paragraph develops its idea fully, and in a manner that readers can follow with ease.

Let's consider these two issues carefully. First, how do we know when an idea is fully developed? If your topic sentence is well written, it should tell you what the paragraph needs to do. If the topic sentence declares, for example, that there are two conflicting impulses at work in a particular fictional character, then the reader will expect the two impulses to be defined and illustrated. It might take two paragraphs to do this; it might take one. The decision will depend on how important this matter is to the discussion. If the point is important, you'll take your time, and (more likely than not) you'll use at least two paragraphs. In this case a topic sentence might be understood as controlling not only a paragraph but an entire section of text.

When you've written a paragraph, ask yourself the following questions:

Do I have enough evidence to support this paragraph's idea?

Do I have too much evidence?

Does this evidence clearly support the assertion that I'm making in this paragraph, or am I stretching it?

If I'm stretching it, what can I do to convince the reader that this stretch is worth making?

Am I repeating myself in this paragraph?

Have I defined all of the paragraph's important terms?

Can I say, in a nutshell, what the purpose of this paragraph is?

Has the paragraph fulfilled that purpose?

ARRANGEMENT

Equally important to the idea of a paragraph's development is the matter of the paragraph's arrangement. Paragraphs are arranged differently for different purposes. For example, if you're writing a paper about a film's history and wish to summarize a sequence of events, you'll likely want to arrange the information chronologically. If you're writing a paper in which you want to describe the composition or setting of a particular shot or scene, perhaps you'll choose to arrange the information spatially. If you're writing a paper about the elements of a film that make it stand out from other movies of a similar type, you might want to arrange your ideas by working from the specific to the general—and so on. The point is to think about what purpose you want the paragraph to serve, and then to come up with an organizational strategy that will help your paragraph to achieve that purpose.

COHERENCE

So you have your thesis, your topic sentences, and truckloads of evidence to support the whole lot. You've spent three days writing your paragraphs, making sure that each paragraph argues one point and that this point is well supported with evidence. But when you read the essay back to yourself, you feel a profound sense of disappointment. Though you've followed your outline, the essay just doesn't seem to hold together. It could be that you have a problem with coherence.

A lack of coherence is easy to diagnose but not so easy to cure. An incoherent essay doesn't seem to flow. Its arguments are hard to understand. The reader has to double back again and again in order to follow the gist of the argument. Something has gone wrong. What?

To improve cohesion in your paper, look for the following issues:

Make sure the grammatical subjects of your sentences reflect the real subject of your paragraph. Underline the subjects of all the sentences in the paragraph. Do these subjects match the paragraph's subject in most cases? Or have you put the paragraph's subject into another, less important part of the sentence? Remember that the reader understands an idea's importance according to where in the sentence you place it. If your main idea is hidden as an object of a preposition in a subordinate clause, do you really think your reader is going to follow what you're trying to say? For instance, consider the following paragraph about the way sound is used in *Apocalypse Now*. The grammatical subject of each sentence is underlined.

> Many **situations** occur in *Apocalypse Now* in which sound is the main means by which we understand characters' psychology. An excellent **example** is the scene when Sgt. Willard is in a hotel room in Hanoi. The Doors' **song** "The End" provides a sound track for Willard's psychological breakdown and Vietnam's insanity, while the sound of a fan over his head blends menacingly with

> the sound of helicopters and the sounds of war. One **shot** in this sequence shows Willard screaming, but we don't hear the scream in the sound mix, and this silence makes Willard's desperation even more palpable.

Look at the four subjects: "situations," "example," "song," and "shot." Of these, only "song" is clearly related to the topic of the paragraph. Now consider this revised paragraph:

> Many times in *Apocalypse Now*, **sound** is the means by which we understand the characters' psychology. In one scene, the rhythmic **pulsing** of a ceiling fan over Sgt. Willard's head blends menacingly with the sounds of helicopters and of war, while The Doors' song "The End" provides a sound track for Willard's psychological breakdown and Vietnam's insanity. The **silence** that accompanies Sgt. Willard's scream near the end of the scene makes his desperation even more palpable.

Look at the subjects here: "sound," "pulsing," and "silence." The paragraph's string of related subjects keeps the reader focused on the topic and creates a paragraph that flows more naturally and seems much more coherent than the first one.

Make sure the grammatical subjects are consistent. Again, look at the grammatical subjects of all your sentences. How many different subjects do you find? If you have too many different sentence subjects, your paragraph will be hard to follow.

Make sure your sentences look backward as well as forward. For a paragraph to be coherent, each sentence should begin by linking itself firmly to the sentence that preceded it. If the link between sentences does not seem firm, use an introductory clause or phrase to connect one idea to the other.

Follow the principle of moving from old to new. If you put the old information at the beginning of the sentence and the new information at the end, you accomplish two things: first, you ensure that your readers are on solid ground, moving from the familiar to the unknown; second, because we tend to give emphasis to what comes at the end of a sentence, readers rightfully perceive that the new information is more important than the old.

Use repetition to create a sense of unity. Repeating key words and phrases at appropriate moments will give your readers a sense of coherence in your work. But don't overdo it; you'll risk sounding redundant.

Use transition markers wisely. Sometimes you'll need to announce to your readers a turn in your argument, or you'll want to emphasize one point, or you'll want to make clear a particular relationship in time. In all these cases you'll want to use transition markers. Some examples follow:

- **To give an example:** *for example, for instance*
- **To present a list:** *first, second, third, next, then*
- **To show that you have more to say:** *in addition, furthermore, moreover*
- **To indicate similarity:** *also, likewise, similarly*
- **To show an exception:** *but, however, nevertheless, on the other hand*
- **To show cause and effect:** *accordingly, consequently, therefore, because*
- **To emphasize:** *indeed, in fact, of course*
- **To conclude:** *finally, in conclusion, in the end*

Introductions and Conclusions

Introductions and conclusions are among the most challenging of all paragraphs. Why? Because they must do more than state a topic sentence and offer support. Introductions and conclusions must synthesize and provide context for your entire argument, and they must also make the proper impression on your readers.

The introduction is your chance to get readers interested in your subject. Accordingly, the tone of the paragraph has to be just right. You want to inform, but not to the point of being dull; you want to intrigue, but not to the point of being vague; you want to take a strong stance, but not to the point of alienating readers. Pay attention to the nuances of your tone. Seek out a second reader if you're not sure that you've managed to get the tone you want.

Equally important to the tone of the introduction is that it needs to "place" your argument into a larger context. Some strategies follow:

Announce your topic broadly; then declare your particular take. For example, if you're interested in talking about the symbolism of Fellini's films, you might (1) begin by saying that Fellini's symbolism has posed a problem for many of his critics, (2) provide a quick definition of the problem as others have defined it, and (3) declare your thesis (which states your own position on the matter).

Provide any background material important to your argument. If you're interested in exploring how events in the 1960s influenced the work of Oliver Stone, then in your introduction you'll want to provide for the reader, in broad strokes, a description of the sixties. Don't include irrelevant details in your description; instead, emphasize those aspects of the culture (the assassination of John F. Kennedy, the war in Vietnam) that might have most influenced Stone.

Define key terms as you intend to make use of them in your argument. If, for example, you're writing a paper on cinema verité, it is absolutely essential that you define the term for your reader. For example, how do you understand the term *verité*? How do you understand *reality*? Begin with a definition of terms, and from there work toward the declaration of your argument.

Use an anecdote or a quotation. Sometimes you'll find a terrific story or quotation that seems to reflect the main point of your paper. Don't be afraid to begin with it. Be sure, however, that you tie that story or quotation clearly and immediately to your main argument. Also, be sure that this anecdote or quotation is really the best way to begin—too often students use an anecdote or quotation to catch the reader's attention, but the anecdote or quotation isn't clearly relevant to the point of the paper, or it sets a tone that is not academic.

Acknowledge your opponents and/or those with whom you align. When you're writing a paper about a controversial matter, you might wish to begin by summarizing the point of view of your adversaries. Conversely, you might summarize the scholarship with which you align. Then state your own position in opposition to theirs. Either way, place yourself clearly in the ongoing conversation.

Remember, the introduction is the first impression that your argument will make on the reader. Take special care with your sentences so that they'll be interesting. Also take the time to consider who your readers are and what background they will bring with them to their reading. If your readers are very knowledgeable about the subject, you will not need to provide a lot of background information. If your readers are less knowledgeable, you will need to be more careful about defining terms.

Finally, you might want to consider writing the introduction after you've written the rest of the paper. Many writers find that they have a better grip on their subject once they've done a first draft. This "better grip" helps them craft an introduction that is sure-footed, persuasive, interesting, and clear. But be careful. Any changes that you make to an introduction and/or a thesis statement will affect the paper that follows. Simply adding the new introductory paragraph will not produce a completed paper.

Conclusions are also difficult to write. How do you manage to make the reader feel persuaded by what you've said? Even if the points of your paper are strong, the overall effect of your argument might fall to pieces if the paper as a whole is badly concluded.

Many students end their papers by simply summarizing what has come before. A summary of what the reader has just read is important to the conclusion—particularly if your argument has been complicated or has covered a lot of ground. But a good conclusion will do more. Just as the introduction sought to place the paper in the larger, ongoing conversation about the topic, so should the conclusion insist on returning readers to that ongoing conversation, but with the feeling that they've learned something more. You don't want readers to finish your paper and say "So what?" Admittedly, writing a conclusion isn't easy.

Many of the strategies we've listed for improving introductions can help you improve your conclusions as well. In the conclusion you might do the following:

Return to the ongoing conversation, emphasizing the importance of your own contribution to it.

Consider again the background information with which you began, and illustrate how your argument has shed new light on that information.

Return to the key terms and point out how your essay has added new dimension to their meanings.

Use an anecdote or a quotation that summarizes or reflects your main idea.

Acknowledge your opponents—if only to emphasize that you've countered their positions successfully.

Remember, language is especially important to a conclusion. Your goal in the final sentences is to leave your ideas resonating in the reader's mind. Give the reader something to think about. Make your language ring.

9

Attending to Style

Most of us know good style when we see it—and *hear* it in the mind's ear. We also know when a sentence seems cumbersome to read. However, though we can easily spot beastly sentences, it is not as easy to say why a sentence—especially one that is grammatically correct—isn't working. We look at the sentence, we see that the commas are in the right places, and we find no error to speak of. So why is the sentence so awful? What's gone wrong?

When thinking about what makes a good sentence, put yourself in the reader's place. What is a reader hoping to find in your sentences? Information, yes. Eloquence, surely. But, most important, a reader is looking for clarity. Your reader does not want to wrestle with sentences. She wants to read with ease. She wants to see one idea build on another. She wants to experience, without struggling, the emphasis of your language and the importance of your idea. Above all, she wants to feel that you, the writer, are doing the bulk of the work. In short, she wants to read sentences that are persuasive, straightforward, and clear.[2]

Basic Principles of the Sentence

FOCUS ON ACTORS AND ACTIONS

To understand what makes a good sentence, it's important to understand one principle: a sentence, at its very basic level, is about actors and actions. As such, the subject of a sentence should point clearly to the actor, and the verb of the sentence should describe the important action.

This principle might seem so obvious to you that you don't think it warrants further discussion. But think again. Look at the following sentence, and then try to determine, in a nutshell, what's wrong with it:

> There is a question in the mind of some screenwriters over whether the employment of flashbacks is a sign of weakness in a script.

This sentence has no grammatical errors. But certainly it lumbers along, without any force. What are the actors? What are the actions?

[2] The way of teaching style that is represented here has been greatly influenced by Joseph Williams and his work. For a thorough examination of the fundamental principles of style, see Williams's *Style: Lessons in Clarity and Grace*, 10th ed. (New York: Pearson Longman, 2010).

Now consider the following sentence:

> Some screenwriters question whether flashbacks signify a weak script.

What changes does this sentence make? We can point to the more obvious changes: omitting the empty *there is* phrase, replacing the abstract noun *sign* with the stronger verb *signify*, replacing a second abstract noun *weakness* with the adjective *weak*, omitting all of the prepositions that the abstract nouns require. What principle governs these many changes? Precisely the one mentioned earlier: that the *actors* in a sentence should serve as the sentence's grammatical subjects, and the *actions* should be illustrated forcefully in the sentence's verbs.

Whenever you feel that your prose is confusing or hard to follow, find the actors and the actions of your sentences. Is the actor the subject of your sentence? Is the action related, vividly, in a verb? If not, rewrite your sentences accordingly.

BE CONCRETE

Student writers tend to rely too heavily on abstract nouns: they use *expectation* when the verb *expect* is stronger; they write *evaluation* when *evaluate* is more vivid. So why use an abstract noun when a verb will do better? Many students believe that abstract nouns permit them to sound more "academic." When you write with a lot of abstract nouns, however, you risk confusing your reader. You also end up cornering yourself syntactically. Consider the following:

Nouns often require prepositions. Too many prepositional phrases in a sentence are hard to follow. Verbs, on the other hand, can stand on their own. They're cleaner; they don't box you in. If you need some proof of this claim, consider the following sentence:

> An evaluation of the footage by the director is necessary prior to our editing process.

Notice all of the prepositional phrases that these nouns require. Now look at the following sentence, which uses verbs:

> The director must evaluate the footage before we edit it.

This sentence has fewer nouns and prepositions, and is therefore much easier to read—yet it still conveys all the information found in the prior sentence.

Abstract nouns often invite the *there is* construction. Consider the following sentence:

> There is a method of acting that Konstantin Stanislavsky invented in which acting students are taught about the use of past experiences to bring emotion to their roles.

We might rewrite this sentence as follows:

> Konstantin Stanislavsky invented a method that teaches actors to use past experiences to bring emotion to their roles.

The result, again, is a sentence that is more direct and easier to read.

Abstract nouns are, well, abstract. Using too many abstract nouns will leave your prose seeming ungrounded. Words such as *falsification*, *beauteousness*, and *insubstantiality* sound pompous and vague—which may be exactly what you want, if you're striving for a slightly comic, self-mocking effect. But, by and large, people simply don't talk this way. Instead, use concrete nouns, as well as strong verbs, to convey your ideas. *Lying*, *beauty*, and *flimsiness* reflect the way people really speak; these words point directly to their meanings without drawing undue attention to themselves.

Abstract nouns can obscure your logic. Note how hard it is to follow the line of reasoning in the following sentence (the nouns that might be rewritten as verbs or as adjectives are in boldface):

> **Decisions** with regard to **the dismissal** of actors on the basis of **their unwillingness** to put on weight for a role rest with the director.

Now consider this sentence:

> When actors refuse to gain weight for a role, the director must decide whether or not to dismiss them.

The Exception: When to Use Abstract Nouns

In some instances an abstract noun will be essential to the sentence. Sometimes abstract nouns refer to a previous sentence (e.g., *these arguments, this decision*). Other times they allow you to be more concise (e.g., *her argument* versus *what she argued*). And, in other cases, the abstract noun is a concept important to your argument: freedom, love, revolution, and so on. Still, if you examine your prose, you'll probably find that you overuse abstract nouns. Omitting from your writing those abstract nouns that aren't really necessary makes for leaner, "fitter" prose.

BE CONCISE

One of the most exasperating aspects of reading student texts is that most students don't know how to write concisely. Students use phrases when a single word will do, offer pairs of adjectives and verbs when one is enough, or overwrite, saying the same thing two or three times with the hope that the reader will be impressed by a point worth rephrasing and then rephrasing again.

Stop the madness! It's easy to delete words and phrases from your prose once you've learned to be ruthless about it.

Do you really need words such as *actually, basically, generally*, and so on? If you don't need them, why are they there? Are you using two words where one will do? Isn't the phrase *first and foremost* redundant? What's the point of *future* in *future plans*? And why do you keep saying *"In my opinion"*? Doesn't the reader understand that this is your paper, based on your point of view? Does drawing attention to yourself in this way make your points any stronger—or does it have the opposite effect, coming across as insecurity or as hedging?

Sometimes you won't be able to fix a wordy sentence by simply deleting a few words or phrases. You'll have to rewrite the whole sentence. Take the following sentence, for example:

> Plagiarism is a serious academic offense resulting in punishments that might include suspension or dismissal, profoundly affecting your academic career.

The idea here is simple: *Plagiarism is a serious offense with serious consequences.* Why not simply say so? Don't be afraid to let your reader connect your ideas to the context—at its most pleasurable, good writing gives the reader a sense of collaboration, of being trusted to connect the dots.

BE COHERENT

At this point in discussing style, we move from the sentence as a discrete unit to the way that sentences fit together. Coherence (or the lack of it) is a common problem in student papers.

Sometimes a professor encounters a paper in which all the ideas seem to be there, but they're hard to follow. The prose seems jumbled. The line of reasoning is anything but linear. Couldn't the student have made this paper a bit more readable?

Although coherence is a complicated and difficult matter to address, we can offer a couple of tricks that will help your sentences to "flow." To manage this, follow the simple principle of "old to new." In other words, most of the sentences you write should begin with the old—with something that looks back to the previous sentence. Your sentence should then move on to telling the reader something new. If you do this, your line of reasoning will be easier for readers to follow.

Though this advice sounds simple enough, it is not always easy to follow. Let's dissect the practice so that we can better understand how our sentences might "flow."

Consider, first, the beginnings of sentences. The coherence of your paper depends largely on how well you begin sentences. "Well begun is half done," says Mary Poppins in the film of the same name, and in this case (as in all cases, really) she's right.

Beginning a sentence is hard work. When you begin a sentence, you have three important matters to consider:

1. **Is your topic also the subject of the sentence?** When a sentence lacks coherence, usually it's because the writer has not been careful to ensure that the topic of the sen-

tence is also the grammatical subject of the sentence. If, for instance, you're writing a sentence whose topic is the importance of the close-up in silent films, then the grammatical subject of the sentence should reflect that idea:

A silent-film actor's **facial expressions** were more important to his success than his body language.

If, on the other hand, you bury your topic in a subordinate clause, look what happens:

The rise of the silent-film stars, which came about **because of their facial expressions**, was not due to their control of body language.

The emphasis and focus of the sentence are obscured.

2. **Are the topics/subjects of your sentences consistent?** For a paragraph to be coherent, most of the sentence subjects should be the same. To check for consistency, pick out a paragraph and make a list of its sentence subjects. See if any of the subjects seem out of place. For example, if you're writing a paragraph about the importance of the close-up in a paper on silent films, do most of your sentence subjects reflect that paragraph topic? Or do some of your sentences have other, tangential topics (such as "gestures" or "body language") as the grammatical subject? Although

the full-body comedy of silent film stars such as Charlie Chaplin and Buster Keaton may indeed have a place in your paper on silent films, you will confuse readers if your paragraph's sentence subjects point to too many competing ideas. Revise the sentences (or perhaps the entire paragraph) for coherence.

3. **Have you marked, when appropriate, the transitions between ideas?** Coherence depends on how well you connect a sentence to the one that came before it. You'll want to make solid transitions between your sentences, using words such as *however* or *therefore.* You'll also want to signal to readers whenever, for example, something important or disappointing comes up. In these cases you'll want to use expressions such as *note that* or *unfortunately.* You might also want to indicate time or place in your argument. If so, you'll use transitions such as *then, later, earlier,* or *in the previous paragraph.* Be careful not to overuse transition phrases. Some writers think transition phrases can, all by themselves, direct a reader through an argument. Indeed, sometimes all a paragraph needs is a *however* in order for its argument suddenly to make sense. More often, though, the problem with coherence does not stem from a lack of transition phrases but from the fact that the writer has not articulated, for himself, the connections between his ideas. Don't rely on transition phrases alone to bring sense to muddled prose.

BE EMPHATIC

We've been talking about how sentences begin, but what about how they end?

If the beginnings of sentences must look over their shoulders at what came before, the ends of sentences must forge ahead into new ground. It's the end of a sentence, then, that must be courageous and emphatic. You must construct sentences so that the ends pack the punch.

To write emphatically, follow these principles:

Declare important ideas at the end of a sentence. Shift less important ideas to the front.

Tighten the ends of sentences. Don't trail off into nonsense, don't repeat yourself, and don't qualify what you've just said if you don't have to. Simply make your point and move on.

Use subordinate clauses to house subordinate ideas. Put all the important ideas in main clauses and the less important ideas in subordinate clauses. If you have two ideas of equal importance that you want to express in the same sentence, use parallel constructions or semicolons. These two tricks of the trade are perhaps more useful than any others in balancing equally significant ideas.

BE IN CONTROL

When sentences run on and on, readers know that a writer has lost control. Take command of your sentences. When you read over your paper, look for sentences that never seem to end. Your first impulse might be to take these long sentences and divide them into two (or three or four). This simple solution often works. But sometimes this strategy isn't the most desirable one; it might lead to short, choppy sentences. Moreover, if you always cut your sentences in two, you'll never learn how a sentence can be long and complex without violating the boundaries of good prose.

What do you do when you encounter an overly long sentence? First, consider the point of your sentence. Usually it will have more than one point, and sorting out the points helps to sort out the grammar. Consider carefully the points that you're trying to make, the importance of each point, and the connections between the points. Then try to determine which grammatical structure best serves your purpose.

Are the points of equal importance? Use a coordinating conjunction (*and, but, or*) or a semicolon to join the ideas. Try to use parallel constructions when appropriate.

Are the points of unequal importance? Use subordinate clauses (*although, while, because*, and so on) or relative clauses *(that, which)* to join the ideas, putting the less important idea in the subordinate clause.

Does one point make for an interesting aside? Insert that point between commas, dashes, or even parentheses at the appropriate juncture in the sentence.

Do these ideas belong in the same sentence? If not, create two sentences.

WRITE BEAUTIFULLY

In your career as a writer you will sometimes produce a paper that is well written but could be written better. On this happy occasion, you might wish to turn your attention to such matters as balance, parallel structure, emphasis, rhythm, and word choice. If you're interested in exploring these rhetorical tools, consult one of several excellent style books, such as Joe Williams's *Style: The Basics of Clarity and Grace,* William Strunk Jr. and E. B. White's *The Elements of Style,* or John Trimble's *Writing with Style.* You will find plenty of valuable advice in any one of these sources.

10

Revising Your Work

Why and How to Revise

Most of us who compose on a computer understand revision as an ongoing—even constant—process. Every time you hit the delete key, every time you cut and paste, and every time you take out a comma or exchange one word for another, you're revising.

Real revision, however, is more than making a few changes here and there. Real revision, just as the word implies, calls for *seeing again*; it requires that you open yourself up to the possibility that parts of your paper—even your entire paper—might need to be rethought, and rewritten.

Achieving this state of mind is difficult. First, you might be very attached to what you've written. You might be unwilling to change a word, let alone three or four paragraphs. Second, there's the matter of time: you might sense that the paper needs major work, but it's due tomorrow, or you have an exam in physics, or you're coming down with a cold and know that you need to sleep. Third, you might have difficulty understanding what, exactly, is wrong with your paper. Finally, you might simply be sick and tired of the paper. How can you make another pass through it when exhaustion has you in its grip? Why should you be bothered with (or let yourself be overwhelmed by) the process of revising?

Of course we might convince you that revision is worth the extra effort simply by saying that revising a paper will help you achieve a better grade. A good reader can sense when a piece of writing has been thoroughly considered and reconsidered. This consideration (and here we mean the word in both of its meanings) is not lost on your professor and will be rewarded.

More important than grades, however, is the fact that revising your papers teaches you to be a better writer. Professional writers know that to write is to rewrite. In the revision process you improve your reading skills and your analytical skills. You learn to challenge your own ideas, thus deepening and strengthening your argument. You learn to find the weaknesses in your writing. You may even discover patterns of error or habits of organization that are undermining your papers.

Although revising takes time and energy, it will also help you become a more efficient writer down the road. If, for example, you have discovered through the revision process that you tend to bury your topic sentences in the middle of your paragraphs, you can take this discovery with you as you draft your next paper. You may then be less likely to make that particular mistake again.

We've answered the question "Why should I revise?" The next question, of course, is "How?" There are many different kinds of revising, including the following:

Large-scale revision. Large-scale revision means looking at the entire paper for places where your thinking seems to go awry. You might need to provide evidence, define terms, or add an entirely new step to your reasoning. You might even decide to restructure or rewrite your paper completely if you discover a new idea that intrigues you, or a structure that seems to be more effective than the one you've been using.

Small-scale revision. Small-scale revision needs to happen when you know that a certain part of your paper isn't working. Maybe the introduction needs work. Maybe one part of the argument seems weak. Once you've located the problem, you'll focus on revising that one section of your paper. When you're finished you'll want to reconsider your paper as a whole to make sure that your revisions work in the context of the entire paper.

Editing. Too often students confuse editing with revision. They are not the same processes. Editing is the process of finding minor problems with a text—problems that might easily be fixed by deleting a word or sentence, cutting and pasting a paragraph, and so on. When you edit, you're considering your reader. You might be happy with how you've written your paper, but will your reader find your paper clear, readable, and interesting? How can you rewrite the paper so that it's clearer, more concise, and, most important of all, a pleasure to read?

The very best writers revise their writing in all the ways listed here. To manage these various levels of revision, it's very important that you get an early start on your papers so that you have time to make any substantive, large-scale revisions that might be needed. Good writers also understand that revision is an ongoing process, not necessarily something that you do only after your first draft is complete. You might find, for example, that you're stuck halfway through the first draft of your paper. You decide to take a look at what you have so far. As you read, you find that you've neglected to make a point that is essential to the success of your argument. You revise what you've written, making that point clear. In the end you find that your block, your "stuckness," is gone. Why? Maybe it's gone because what was blocking you in the first place was a hole in your argument. Or maybe it's gone because you gave your brain a break. In any case, stopping to revise in the middle of the drafting process often proves wise.

Developing a Critical Eye

We have yet to address the matter of how a writer knows what she should revise. Developing a critical eye is perhaps the most difficult part of the revision process. But having a critical eye makes you a better writer, reader, and thinker. So it's worth considering carefully how you might learn to see your own work with the objectivity that is essential to successful self-criticism.

The first step in developing a critical eye is to get some distance from your work. If you've planned your writing process well, you'll have left yourself a day or two to take a break. If you don't have this luxury, even an hour of video games or a walk over to the printing center to pick up a hard copy of your draft might be enough to clear your head. Many writers find that their mind keeps working on their papers even while their attention is turned elsewhere. When they return to their work, they bring with them a fresh perspective. They also bring a more open mind.

When you return to your paper, the first thing you'll want to do is consider whether or not the paper as a whole meets your (and your professor's) expectations. Read the paper through without stopping (don't get hung up on one troublesome paragraph). Then ask yourself the following questions:

Did I fulfill the assignment? If the professor gave you instructions for this assignment, reread them and then ask yourself whether you've addressed all of the matters you're expected to address. Does your paper stray from the assignment? If it does, have you worked to make your argument relevant, or are you coming out of left field? If the professor hasn't given you explicit instructions for this paper, you'll still want to take a moment to consider what she or he expects. What books has the professor asked you to read? What position does he or she take toward your topic? Has the professor emphasized a certain method of scholarship (e.g., feminism, Marxism)? Has she or he said anything to you about research methods in his or her discipline? Does your paper seem to fit into the conversation that the professor has been carrying on in class? Have you written something that other students would find relevant and interesting?

Did I say what I intended to say? This question is perhaps the most difficult question you will ask yourself in the revision process. Many of us think that we have indeed said what we intended to say. When we read our papers, we're able to fill in any holes that might exist in our arguments with the information that we have in our minds. The problem is that our readers sometimes don't have this same information in mind. Your challenge in revising your own writing, therefore, is to forget about what you *meant* and see only what you actually *wrote*—the meaning has to be right there in the words on the page. It's very important to think carefully about what you've said—and to think just as carefully about what you haven't said. Ask yourself the following questions: Was I clear? Do I need to define my terms? Has every stage of the argument been articulated clearly? Have I made adequate transitions between my ideas? Is my logic solid—is it there for all to see? If the answer to any of these questions is no, you will want to revise your draft.

What are the strengths of my paper? In order to develop a critical eye, it's just as important to know when you've written well as it is to know when you've written poorly. It helps, therefore, to make a list of what you think you've done well in your draft. It's also helpful to pick out your favorite or strongest paragraph. When you find a good paragraph, sentence, or idea, think about why it's good. You'll not only be gaining an understanding of what it means to write well, but you'll also be giving yourself a pat on the back—something that's very important to do in the revision process.

What are the weaknesses of my paper? Looking for weaknesses isn't as much fun as looking for strengths, but it's necessary to the revision process. Again, try to make a list of what you haven't done well in this paper. Your list should be as specific as you can make it. Instead of writing "problems with paragraphs," you might say "problems with unity in my paragraphs," or, even more specific, "problems with the transitions between paragraphs 3 and 4, and 12 and 13." Also force yourself to determine which paragraph (or sentence) you like least in the paper. Figure out why you don't like it, and work to make it better. Then go back through your paper and look for others similar to it.

Analyzing Your Work

If you've been considering the strengths and weaknesses of your paper, you've already begun to analyze your work. The process of analysis involves breaking down an idea or an argument into its parts and evaluating those parts on their merits. When you analyze your own paper, you're breaking down that paper into its parts and asking yourself whether or not these parts support the paper as you envision it.

The following checklist reiterates our earlier advice. Use it to analyze your whole paper, or to help you figure out what has gone wrong with a particular part of your work.

Consider your introduction:

If you're writing a research paper, does the introduction place your argument in an ongoing conversation?

If you're not writing a research paper, does the introduction establish context?

Does the introduction define all of your key terms?

Does the introduction draw the reader in?

Does the introduction lead the reader clearly to your thesis?

Consider your thesis:

Does the thesis say what you want it to say?

Does the thesis make a point worth considering? Does it answer the question "So what?"

Does the thesis provide the reader with some sense of the paper's structure?

Does the paper deliver what your thesis promises to deliver?

Consider your structure:

Make an outline of the paper you've just written. Does this outline reflect your intentions?

Does this outline make sense, or are there gaps in the logic—places where you've asked your readers to make leaps for which they haven't been prepared?

Is each point in the outline adequately developed?

Is each point equally developed? That is, does your paper seem balanced overall?

Is each point relevant? Interesting?

Underline the thesis sentence and all of the topic sentences. Then cut and paste them together to form a paragraph. Does this paragraph make sense?

Consider your paragraphs:

Does each paragraph have a topic sentence that clearly controls it?

Are the paragraphs internally coherent?

Are the paragraphs externally coherent? That is, have you made adequate transitions between paragraphs? Is each paragraph clearly related to the thesis?

Consider your argument and its logic:

Have you really presented an argument, an assertion worth making, or is your paper merely a series of observations, a summary?

Do you see any holes in your argument, or do you find it convincing?

Have you dealt fairly with the opposition, or have you neglected to mention other possible arguments concerning your topic for fear that they might undermine your own argument?

Have you supplied ample evidence for your arguments?

Consider your conclusion:

Does the conclusion sum up the main point of the paper?

Is the conclusion appropriate, or does it introduce a completely new idea?

Does the language resonate, or does it fall flat?

Have you inflated the language in order to pad a conclusion that is empty and ineffective?

Does the conclusion leave the reader with something to think about?

The final step that you'll want to take before submitting your paper is to make sure that the grammar, spelling, and punctuation throughout the paper are correct and that you've formatted it appropriately. These details may seem frustratingly minor, but errors often cause readers to grow impatient with otherwise well-written essays. So be sure to take the time to carefully proofread your essay.

When you proofread, you need to slow down your reading, allowing your eye to focus on every word, every phrase of your paper. Reading aloud is the most effective way to make yourself see and hear what you actually *wrote*, not just what you *meant*. Remember, a computer spell-checker is not an editor—for example, the spell-checker will see the word "form" as spelled correctly, even if you meant "from." As you read, look for common errors—spelling errors, faulty subject–verb agreement, unclear pronoun antecedents, *its/it's* confusion, *their/there* confusion, and so on. If you have time, get the opinion of a second reader. Treat the proofreading stage as you would a word search or Sudoku puzzle—that is, as a puzzle to be solved. No doubt some errors are lurking in your prose (even professional writers find errors when they proofread their own work). Make it your mission to find and eliminate them.

You'll also want to format the paper correctly. Some instructors provide explicit directions about constructing a title page, choosing a font, setting margins, paginating, footnoting, and so on. Be sure to follow these instructions carefully. If the instructor does not provide directions, consult the *MLA Handbook*—the standard reference for writers in the humanities—for specific advice. Instructors appreciate papers that are not only well written but also beautifully presented. In academic writing, "beauty" equals simplicity: no needless ornamentation, no fancy fonts, and nothing to distract the reader from the sound of your writer's voice and the clarity of your thoughts.

Part III

RESOURCES

Illustrated Glossary of Film Terms

A

aerial-view shot. Also known as *bird's-eye-view shot*. An extreme high-angle shot that is taken from an aircraft or extremely high crane. The aerial-view shot often represents an omniscient point of view.

An aerial-view shot from Alfred Hitchcock's *The Birds* (1963, Alfred J. Hitchcock Productions).

ambient sound. Sound that seems to the viewer to emanate from the ambience (background) of the setting or environment being filmed. Ambient sound is almost always added or enhanced during postproduction.

angle. The perspective from which the camera shoots a figure. If the camera shoots from below the subject's eye level upward, the resulting shot is a *low-angle shot*. If it is positioned above the subject and shooting downward, the resulting shot is a *high-angle shot*.

animation. The process of creating movies using drawings, computer models, and/or photographs of physical objects representing figures and settings. Common methods of animation include stop-motion photography, drawn animation, and computer animation.

antagonist. The character, creature, or force that obstructs or resists the protagonist's pursuit of a goal.

antihero. An outwardly unsympathetic protagonist pursuing a morally objectionable or otherwise undesirable goal.

aperture. An adjustable diaphragm that limits the amount of light passing through the lens of a camera. See *iris*.

art director. The person responsible for transforming the production designer's vision into a reality on the screen, assessing the staging requirements for a production, and arranging for and supervising the work of the members of the art department.

1.375:1

Three common aspect ratios: 1.33:1 (the "Academy" ratio); 1.85:1 (U.S. widescreen); and 2.35:1 (Cinemascope widescreen), as seen in these scenes from *The Grand Budapest Hotel* (2014, American Empirical Pictures and Indian Paintbrush).

1.85:1

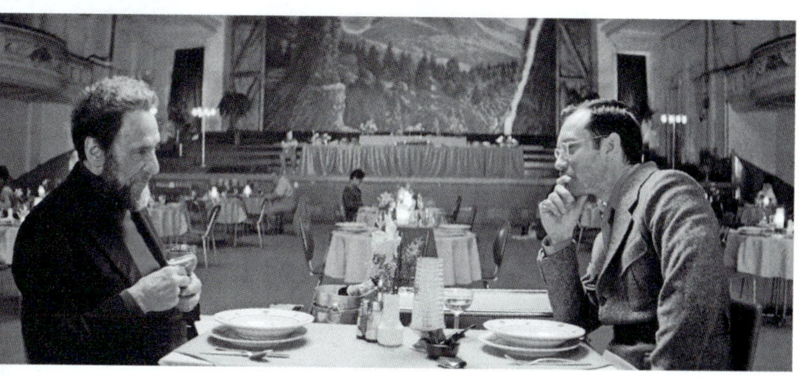

2.35:1

aspect ratio. The relationship between the film frame's two dimensions: the width of the image related to its height.

asynchronous sound. Sound that comes from a source apparent in the image but that is not precisely matched temporally with the actions occurring in that image.

auteurism. A film theory based on the idea that the director is the sole "author" of a movie. The application of auteurism frequently takes two forms: a judgment of the whole body of a film director's work (not individual films) based on style, and a classification of great directors based on a hierarchy of directorial styles.

axis of action. An imaginary line connecting two figures in a scene that defines the 180-degree space within which the camera can record shots of those figures. See *180-degree system*.

B

backlight. Also known as *rim light*. Lighting positioned behind the subject, used to create highlights on the subject as a means of separating it from the background. When the subject is positioned directly between the backlight and the camera, the subject is thrown into silhouette. Using shadows to eliminate recognizable surface detail abstracts the character, which can make him or her (or it) more frightening or impressive, depending on the context of the story at that moment.

An example of backlighting used to create a silhouette from *Citizen Kane* (1941, Mercury Productions).

backstory. A fictional history behind the cinematic narrative that is presented onscreen. Elements of the backstory can be hinted at in a movie, presented through narration, or not revealed at all.

bird's-eye-view shot. See *aerial-view shot*.

blocking. The actual physical relationships among figures and settings. Also, the process during rehearsal of establishing those relationships.

boom. A pole-like mechanical device used to position the microphone outside the camera frame, but as close as possible to speaking actors.

C

cameo. A small but significant role often played by a famous actor.

camera operator. The member of the production crew who operates the camera under the supervision of the director of photography.

casting. The process of choosing and hiring actors for a movie.

cel. A transparent sheet of celluloid or similar plastic on which drawings or lettering may be made for use in animation or titles.

CGI. Computer-generated imagery. See *visual effects*.

character. An essential element of film narrative; any of the beings who play functional roles within the plot, either acting or being acted on. Characters can be any of the following: flat or round; major, minor, or marginal; protagonists or antagonists.

characterization. The process of developing a character in a movie. Characterization is the collaborative result of the creative efforts of the screenwriter, the director, and the actor.

character POV. A point of view (POV) that is captured by a shot made with the camera close to the line of sight of one character (or other figure capable of sight), showing what that person (or figure) would be seeing of the action. Compare *omniscient POV* and *group POV.*

character role. An actor's part that represents a distinctive character type (sometimes a stereotype): for example, society leader, ingenue, mobster, femme fatale, and so on.

chiaroscuro. The use of deep gradations and subtle variations of light and dark within an image. See *low-key lighting.*

A shot from Stanley Kubrick's *The Killing* (1956, Harris-Kubrick Productions) in the chiaroscuro style.

cinematic language. The accepted systems, methods, or conventions by which the movies communicate with the viewer.

cinematic time. The passage of time within a movie, as conveyed and manipulated by editing.

cinematography. The process of lighting, framing, and capturing moving images on film stock or a digital medium.

climax. The highest point of conflict in a conventional narrative; the moment of the protagonist's ultimate attempt to attain the goal by overcoming the final obstacle. Compare *crisis.*

closed frame. An approach to framing a shot that implies that neither characters nor objects may enter or leave the frame—rendering them hemmed in and constrained. Compare *open frame.*

close-up (CU). A shot that often shows a part of the body filling the frame—traditionally a face, but possibly a hand, eye, or mouth.

codec. A specialized digital format that compresses digital image information into manageably sized files for editing and viewing. Like their film-stock counterparts, different codecs capture light, color, contrast, and depth of field in different ways, so digital cinematographers exercise the same care

A closed-frame shot from Akira Kurosawa's *Ikiru* (1952, Toho Company) shows a government bureaucrat literally framed and trapped by the books and papers in his office.

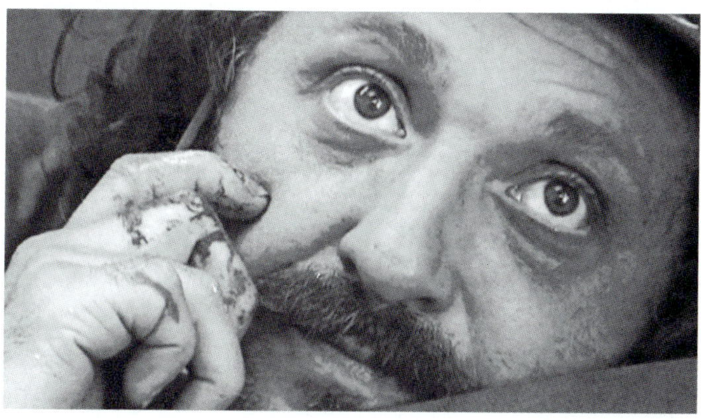

A close-up of Thierry Guetta (aka "Mr. Brainwash") from Banksy's *Exit Through the Gift Shop* (2010, Paranoid Pictures).

when selecting digital formats as those shooting film use when choosing a film stock. Compare *film stock.*

composition. The organization, distribution, balance, and general relationship of stationary objects and figures, as well as of light, shade, line, and color, within the frame.

content. The subject of an artwork. Compare *form.*

continuity editing. A style of editing that seeks to achieve smoothness, sequential flow, and the temporal and spatial orientation of viewers (i.e., the telling of a story as clearly and coherently as possible). Compare *discontinuity editing.*

coverage. The use of a variety of shots of a scene—taken from multiple angles, distances, and perspectives—to provide the director and editor with a greater choice of editing options during postproduction.

crane shot. A shot that is created by movement of a camera mounted on an elevating arm (crane) which in turn is mounted on a vehicle that, if shooting requires it, can move on its own power or be pushed along tracks.

crisis. In a conventional narrative structure, the final, seemingly insurmountable obstacle encountered by the protagonist in pursuit of the goal. Compare *climax.*

A student film crew uses a small crane-like device, called a "jib arm," to shoot a crane shot (photo courtesy of Adam Alphin).

crosscutting. Also called *parallel editing*. Editing that cuts between two or more lines of action, often implied to be occurring at the same time but in different locations.

cut. (a) The act of an editor selecting an in point and an out point of a shot as part of the editing process. (b) A direct change from one shot to another as a result of cutting; that is, the precise point at which shot A ends and shot B begins. (c) An edited version of a scene or film, as in a "rough cut."

cutting on action. Also called a *match-on-action cut*. An editing technique that smoothes the transition between shots portraying a single action from different camera angles. The action portrayed begins in one shot and continues into the next shot, thus implying a continuous action.

D

decor. The color and textures of the interior decoration, furniture, draperies, and curtains of a set.

deep-focus cinematography. In a deep-space composition, the process of rendering the figures on all planes (background, middle ground, and foreground) in focus.

deep-space composition. An approach to composition within the frame that places figures in all three planes (background, middle ground, and foreground) of the frame, thus creating an illusion of depth. Deep-space composition is often, though not always, shot with deep-focus cinematography.

A classic scene using both deep-space composition and deep-focus cinematography from Orson Welles's *Citizen Kane* (1941, Mercury Productions).

depth of field. The portion of the space in front of a camera and its lens in which objects are in apparent sharp focus.

design. The process by which the look of the settings, props, lighting, and actors is determined. Set design, decor, prop selection, lighting setup, costuming, makeup, and hairstyle design all play a role in shaping the overall design.

diegesis. (adj. *diegetic*) The total world of a story—the events, characters, objects, settings, and sounds that form the world in which the story occurs.

diegetic element. An element—an event, character, object, setting, or sound—that is implied to be part of the cinematic world in which a movie's narrative occurs. Compare *nondiegetic element.*

digital animation. Also known as *computer animation.* Animation that employs computer software to create the images used in the animation process (as opposed to analog techniques that rely on stop-motion photography, hand-drawn cels, etc.).

direct narration. A form of narration in which an onscreen character looks and speaks directly to the audience.

director. The person who (a) determines and realizes on the screen an artistic vision of the screenplay, (b) casts the actors and directs their performances, (c) works closely with the production designer in creating the look of the film, including the choice of locations, (d) oversees the work of the cinematographer and other crucial production personnel, and (e) in most cases supervises all postproduction activity, especially the editing.

discontinuity editing. A style of editing—less widely used than continuity editing, often but not exclusively in experimental films—that joins shots A and B in ways that upset the viewer's expectations and cause momentary disorientation or confusion. The juxtaposition of shots in films edited for discontinuity can often seem abrupt and unmotivated, but the meanings that arise from such discordant editing often transcend the meanings of the individual shots that have been joined together.

dissolve. Also known as *lap dissolve.* A transitional device in which shot B, superimposed, gradually appears over shot A and begins to replace it at midpoint in the transition. Dissolves usually indicate the passing of time. Compare *fade-in/fade-out*.

documentary film. A film that purports to be nonfictional. Documentary films take many forms, including the following:

> **factual film** A documentary film that usually presents people, places, or processes in a straightforward way

that is intended to entertain and instruct without unduly influencing audiences.

expository documentary An approach to documentary filmmaking that uses formal elements, a script prepared in advance, and an authoritative narrator to explain the subject matter to the viewer.

observational documentary An approach to documentary filmmaking that seeks to immerse the viewer in an experience as close as is cinematically possible to witnessing events as an invisible observer. Observational documentaries typically rely entirely on b-roll, and eliminate as many other signs of mediation as possible.

participatory documentary An approach to nonfiction filmmaking in which the filmmaker interacts with the subjects and situations being recorded, and thus becomes part of the film.

performative documentary An approach to nonfiction filmmaking related to participatory documentary. The filmmaker's interaction with the subject matter is deeply personal, and often emotional. In a performative documentary, the filmmaker's experience is central to the way in which viewers engage with and understand the subject matter.

persuasive film A documentary film concerned either with presenting a particular perspective on social issues, or with corporate and governmental injustice.

> **propaganda film** A documentary film that systematically disseminates deceptive or distorted information.
>
> **reflexive documentary** An approach to documentary filmmaking that explores and sometimes critiques the documentary form itself. The documentary production process becomes part of the experience in ways that may challenge viewer expectations of nonfiction-filmmaking conventions. Compare *narrative film*.

dolly. A wheeled support for a camera that allows the camera to move smoothly and noiselessly during moving camera shots. Dollies often run on tracks.

A dolly running on tracks during the filming of *The Sopranos* (1999–2007, Home Box Office; photo courtesy of picture-alliance /Newscom).

dolly in. Slow movement of the camera toward a subject, making the subject appear larger in the frame. It is often used to express a character's realization or epiphany.

dolly out. Movement of the camera away from a subject. It is often used for slow disclosure—a technique that uses camera movement to allow new information into the frame that expands or changes the viewer's initial interpretation of the subject or situation.

dolly shot. Also known as *traveling shot*. A shot taken by a camera fixed to a wheeled support called a dolly. When the dolly runs on tracks, the shot is called a tracking shot.

duration. A quantity of time. In any movie, we can identify three specific kinds of duration: *story duration* (the time that the entire narrative arc—whether explicitly presented onscreen or not—is implied to have taken); *plot duration* (the time that the events explicitly shown onscreen are implied to have taken); and *screen duration* (the actual time that has elapsed to present the movie's plot, i.e., the movie's running time).

Dutch-angle shot. Also known as *Dutch shot* or *oblique-angle shot*. A shot in which the camera is tilted from its normal horizontal and vertical positions so that it is no longer straight, giving the viewer the impression that the world in the frame is out of balance.

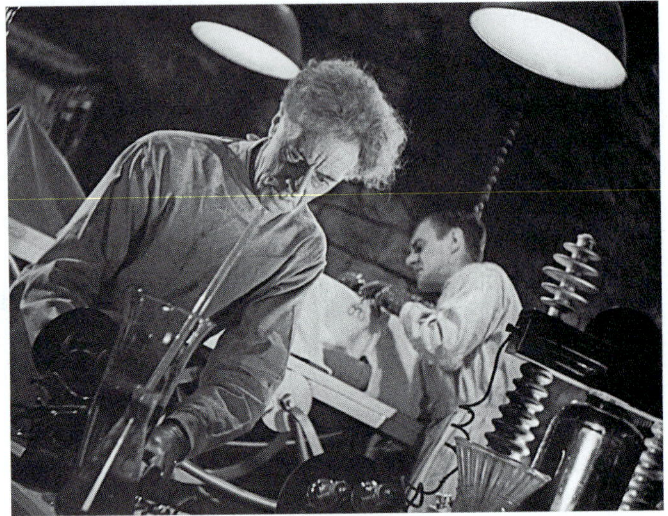

A Dutch-angle shot from James Whale's *Bride of Frankenstein* (1935, Universal Pictures).

E

editing. The process by which the editor combines and coordinates individual shots into a cinematic whole; the basic creative force of cinema.

ellipsis. An omission of time—the time that separates one shot from another—to create dramatic or comic impact.

establishing shot. A shot whose purpose is to briefly establish the viewer's sense of the setting of a scene—the relationship of figures in that scene to the environment around them. This shot is often, but not always, an *extreme long shot*.

An establishing shot from *The King's Speech* (2010, UK Film Council and See-Saw Films) shows us the exterior of a building, which is the implied setting for the interior scene that follows.

experimental film. Also known as *avant-garde film*. Films that employ innovative techniques to defy convention, subvert expectation, and even challenge their own artifice. In his essay "Naming, and Defining, Avant-Garde or Experimental Film," cinema scholar Fred Camper outlined six criteria which summarize the characteristics that most experimental films share:

1. *Experimental films are not commercial.* They are made by single filmmakers (or collaborative teams consisting of, at most, a few artists) for very low budgets and with no expectation of financial gain.
2. *Experimental films are personal.* They reflect the creative vision of a single artist who typically conceives, writes, directs, shoots, and edits the movie with minimal contributions by other filmmakers or technicians. Experimental film credits are short.

3. *Experimental films do not conform to conventional expectations of story and narrative cause and effect.*
4. *Experimental films exploit the possibilities of the cinema* and, by doing so, often reveal (and revel in) tactile and mechanical qualities of motion pictures that conventional movies seek to obscure. Most conventional narrative films are constructed to make audiences forget that they are watching a movie, whereas many experimental films repeatedly remind the viewer of this fact. They embrace innovative techniques that call attention to, question, and even challenge their own artifice.
5. *Experimental films critique culture and the media.* From their position outside the mainstream, they often comment on (and intentionally frustrate) viewer expectations of what a movie should be.
6. *Experimental films invite individual interpretation.* Like abstract expressionist paintings, they resist the kind of accessible and universal meaning that is found in conventional narrative and documentary films.

explicit meaning. Meaning that a movie presents on its surface. Compare *implicit meaning.*

external sound. A form of diegetic sound, audible to characters in the scene and to viewers, that comes from a place within the world of the story, but the source of which we do not see. Compare *internal sound.*

extra. An actor who appears in a nonspeaking or crowd role and receives no screen credit.

extreme close-up (XCU). A very close shot of a particular detail, such as a person's eye, a ring on a finger, or a watch face.

extreme long shot (XLS). A shot that is typically photographed far enough away from the subject for the subject to be too small to be recognized, except through the context we see, which usually includes a wide view of the location, as well as general background information. When it is used to

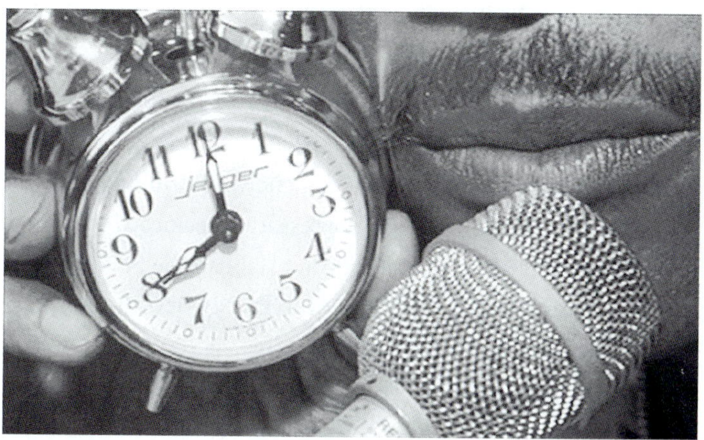

An extreme close-up from Spike Lee's *Do the Right Thing* (1989, 40 Acres and a Mule Filmworks).

provide such informative context, the extreme long shot is also referred to as an *establishing shot*.

eye-level shot. An angle in which the camera is positioned at the eye level of the subject—the standard camera angle used for most shots. If the camera is functioning as narrator, the eye-level angle functions as a neutral view of the action onscreen. If the shot represents the point of view of a character, the eye level is a natural angle to represent how and what that character sees. Camera angles take on a wider range of expressive meanings as soon as the filmmakers deviate from this "normal and neutral" viewpoint.

eye-line match cut. An editing transition that shows us what a particular character is looking at. The cut joins two shots: (a) the character's face, with his or her eyes clearly visible; and then (b) whatever the character was looking at. When the second shot is of another character looking back at the character in the first shot, the resulting reciprocal eye-line match cut, and the cuts that follow, establish the two characters' proximity and interaction, even if only one character is visible onscreen at any one time.

An eye-level shot from John Huston's *The Maltese Falcon* (1941, Warner Bros.).

Successive eye-line match cuts in *Now, Voyager* (1942, Warner Bros.) link the gazes of Bette Davis and Paul Henreid, thus accentuating the intimacy of an emotional turning point in the film.

F

fade-in/fade-out. Transitional devices in which a shot fades in from a black field on black-and-white film or from a color field on color film, or fades out to a black field (or a color field). Compare *dissolve.*

fast motion. Cinematographic technique that accelerates action onscreen. It is achieved by filming the action at a rate less than the normal 24 frames per second (fps). When the shot is then played back at the standard 24 fps, cinematic time proceeds at a more rapid rate than the real action that took place in front of the camera. Compare *slow motion.*

fill light. Lighting positioned at the opposite side of the camera from the key light and used to fill in the shadows created by the brighter key light. Fill light may also come from a reflector board.

film stock. Celluloid used to record movies. Different film stocks capture light, color, contrast, and depth of field in different ways, so cinematographers exercise care when selecting a film stock. Compare *codec.*

film-stock speed. Also known as *film speed* or *exposure index.* The rate at which film must move through the camera to correctly capture an image; very fast film requires little light to capture and fix the image; very slow film requires a lot of light.

film theory. Evaluating movies from a particular intellectual or ideological perspective.

first-person narration. Narration by an actual character in the movie. Compare *voice-over narration*.

flashback. A manipulation of cinematic time in which the action cuts from the present within the narrative to a past event, which may or may not have already appeared in the movie either directly or through inference. Compare *flash-forward*.

flash-forward. A manipulation of cinematic time in which the action cuts from the present within the narrative to a future time in which, for example, an omniscient point of view (POV) might reveal directly, or a character might imagine, from his or her point of view, what is going to happen. Compare *flashback*.

flat character. A relatively uncomplicated character that exhibits few distinct traits and that does not change significantly as the story progresses. Compare *round character*.

floodlight. A lamp that produces soft (diffuse) light. Compare *focusable spotlight*.

focal length. The distance from the optical center of a lens to the focal point (the film plane that the cameraperson wants to keep in focus) when the lens is focused at infinity. Focal length affects a number of visual elements, including depth of field and perspective—the appearance of depth. Focal length also influences our perception of the size, scale, and movement of the subject being shot.

focusable spotlight. A lamp that produces hard, mirrorlike light that can be directed to precise locations. Compare *floodlight*.

A focusable spotlight is used in this scene from Billy Wilder's *Some Like It Hot* (1959, Ashton Productions, The Mirisch Company) to highlight Marilyn Monroe's face and to act as a provocative virtual neckline.

Foley sound. A sound belonging to a special category of sound effects, invented in the 1930s by Jack Foley, a sound technician at Universal Studios. Technicians known as Foley artists create these sounds in specially equipped studios, where they use a variety of props and other equipment to simulate sounds such as footsteps in the mud, jingling car keys, or cutlery hitting a plate.

form. The means by which a subject is expressed. The form for poetry is words; for drama, it is speech and action; for movies, it is pictures and sound; and so on. Compare *content*.

formal analysis. Film analysis that examines how a scene or sequence uses formal elements—narrative, mise-en-scène, cinematography, editing, sound, and so on—to convey story, mood, and meaning.

format. When referring to film stock, also called gauge, the dimensions of the film stock and its perforations, and the size and shape of the image frame as seen on the screen. Formats extend from Super 8mm through 70mm (and beyond into such specialized formats as IMAX), but they are generally limited to three standard gauges: Super 8mm, 16mm, and 35mm. In reference to digital cinematography, format may refer to a specific codec or digital sensor.

frame. (a) A still photograph that, recorded in rapid succession with other still photographs, creates a motion picture. (b) The borders of a motion picture, within which formal elements are composed.

framing. The process by which the cinematographer determines what will appear within the borders of the moving image (the frame) during a shot.

freeze-frame. Also known as *stop-frame* or *hold-frame.* A still image within a movie, created by repetitive printing in the laboratory of the same frame so that it can be seen without movement for whatever length of time the filmmaker desires.

full-body shot. See *long shot.*

FX. See *special effects.*

G

gauge. See *format.*

genre. The categorization of narrative films by form, content, or both. Examples of genres include musical, science fiction, horror, and western.

goal. A narratively significant objective pursued by the protagonist.

graphic match cut. A match cut in which the similarity between shots A and B is in the shape and form of the figures pictured in each shot. The shape, color, or texture of the two figures matches across the edit, providing continuity.

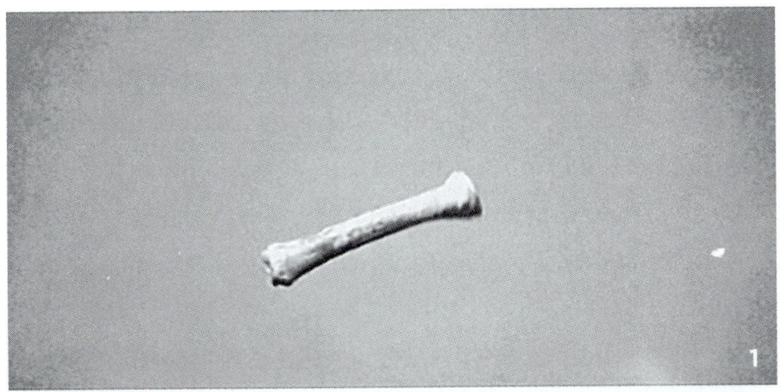

A classic graphic match cut from Stanley Kubrick's *2001: A Space Odyssey* (1968, Metro-Goldwyn Mayer) that first shows a bone [1] that has just been thrown into the air by an ape man, followed by a space ship [2] floating in outer space.

group POV. A point of view (POV) captured by a shot that shows what a group of characters would see, but at the group's level, not from the much higher omniscient point of view. Compare *character POV.*

H

handheld shot. A shot taken from a camera held by a camera operator either on the shoulder or in the hands. Because news and documentary filmmakers rely on the flexibility of the handheld camera to cover unpredictable ongoing events, its unstable look is often associated with documentary realism. In some contexts, the handheld camera's instability is used to convey chaotic situations or the perspective of a running character.

high-angle shot. Also known as *high shot* or *down shot*. A shot that is made with the camera above the action and that typically implies the observer's sense of superiority to the subject being photographed. Compare *low-angle shot*.

high-key lighting. Lighting that produces an image with very little contrast between darks and lights, producing an even, flat illumination of the subject. Compare *low-key lighting.*

hold-frame. See *freeze-frame.*

A high-angle shot from Fritz Lang's *M* (1931, Nero Film AG).

This shot of Grace Kelly in Alfred Hitchcock's *Rear Window* (1954, Patron Inc.) is the result of high-key lighting.

I

implicit meaning. An association, connection, or inference that a viewer makes on the basis of the *explicit meaning* conveyed by the form and content of the film. Lying below the surface of explicit meaning, implicit meaning is closest to our everyday sense of the word *meaning*.

improvisation. (a) Actors' extemporization—that is, delivering lines based only loosely on the written script or without the preparation that comes with studying a script before rehearsing it. (b) "Playing through" a moment—that is, making up lines to keep scenes going when actors forget their written lines, stumble on lines, or have some other mishap.

in-camera effect. A special effect that is created in the production camera (the regular camera used for shooting the rest of the film) on the original negative. Examples include *slow motion* and *fast motion*. Compare *laboratory effect* and *CGI*.

inciting incident. The narrative event or situation that presents the protagonist with a goal that sets the rest of the narrative in motion.

intercutting. The insertion of shots into a scene in a way that interrupts the narrative. Examples of intercutting include flashbacks, flash-forwards, shots depicting a character's thoughts, shots depicting events from earlier or later in the plot, and associative editing that inserts shots to create symbolic or thematic meaning through juxtaposition.

internal sound. A form of diegetic sound that we are to assume is heard (or imagined) by one character but is not audible to other characters. Compare *external sound.*

intertitles. Words—printed or handwritten—inserted into the body of a film in between shots to provide additional exposition or dialogue. Not in common usage today, but used extensively in silent movies.

iris. (a) A circular cutout made with a mask that creates a frame within a frame. (b) An adjustable diaphragm that limits the amount of light passing through the lens of a camera See *aperture.*

iris shot. Optical wipe effect in which the wipe line is a circle; named after the iris of a camera. The iris-in begins with a small circle, which expands to a partial or full image; the iris-out begins with a large circle, which contracts to a smaller circle or total blackness.

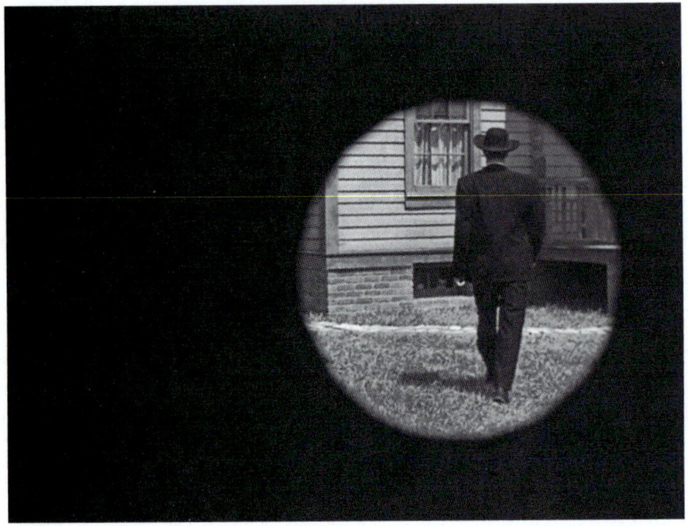

An iris shot from Charles Laughton's *The Night of the Hunter* (1955, Paul Gregory Productions).

J

jump cut. The removal of a portion of a continuous shot, resulting in an instantaneous advance in the action—a sudden, perhaps illogical, often disorienting ellipsis.

K

key light. Also known as *main light* or *source light*. The key light is the primary source of illumination in a shot. Positioned to one side of the camera, it creates deep shadows, which are modified by the fill light.

kinesis. The aspect of composition that takes into account everything that moves on the screen.

L

laboratory effect. A special effect that is created in the laboratory through processing and printing. Compare *in-camera effect* and *CGI*.

lens. The piece of transparent material in a camera that focuses the image on the film or digital processor. Lenses are classified by focal length. See *short-focal-length lens*, *middle-focal-length lens*, *long-focal-length lens*, and *zoom lens*.

lighting ratio. The relationship and balance between illumination and shadow—the balance between key light and fill light. If the ratio is high, shadows are deep; the result is called *low-key lighting*. If the ratio is low, shadows are faint or nonexistent and illumination is even; the result is called *high-key lighting*.

long-focal-length lens. Also known as *telephoto lens*. A lens that flattens the space and depth of an image and thus distorts perspectival relations. Compare *middle-focal-length lens*, *short-focal-length lens*, and *zoom lens*.

This shot from Stanley Kubrick's *Barry Lyndon* (1975, *Hawk Films*) was shot with a telephoto lens. The many rows of soldiers are compressed by the long-focal-length lens, flattening the depth of the scene.

A long shot from Orson Welles's *Citizen Kane* (1941, Mercury Productions).

long shot (LS). Also known as *full-body shot*. A shot that shows the full human body, usually filling the frame, and some of its surroundings.

long take. Also known as *sequence shot*. An uninterrupted shot that lasts significantly longer than a conventional shot. Long takes may be as short as one minute or as long as an entire feature film. There are two basic approaches to the long take: (a) those that exploit the mobile frame; and (b) those that hold the viewer in a state of relative stasis.

low-angle shot. Also known as *low shot*. A shot that is made with the camera below the action and that typically places the observer in a position of inferiority. Compare *high-angle shot*.

A low-angle shot from Spike Lee's *Do the Right Thing* (1989, 40 Acres and a Mule Filmworks).

A shot from Chad Stahelski's *John Wick* (2014, Thunder Road Pictures) makes use of low-key lighting.

low-key lighting. An approach to lighting a subject in which little or no fill light is used to moderate the depth of shadows created by the key light. Low key lighting features deep shadows and high contrasts between illumination and shadow. Compare *high-key lighting*.

M

major role. Also known as *main role, featured role*, or *leading role*. A role that is a principal agent in helping to move the plot forward. Whether movie stars or newcomers, actors playing major roles appear in many scenes and—ordinarily, but not always—receive screen credit preceding the title. Compare *minor role*.

mask. An opaque sheet of metal, paper, or plastic with a cutout (e.g., a circular cutout, known as an iris), which is placed in front of the camera and admits light through that cutout to a specific area of the frame, to create a frame within a frame.

master shot. A shot that covers the action of a scene in one continuous take. Master shots are usually composed as *long shots* so that all of the characters in the scene are onscreen during the action of the scene. These shots are used as a unifying shot in scenes edited from *coverage*—multiple angles and shot types covering the same action—that gives the editor the freedom to select the best possible viewpoint for each dramatic moment.

match cut. A cut that preserves continuity between two shots. Several kinds of match cuts exist, including the *eye-line match cut*, the *graphic match cut*, and the *match-on-action cut*.

match-on-action cut. Also called *cutting on action*. A *match cut* that shows us the continuation of a character's or object's motion through space without actually showing us the entire action. This is a fairly routine editorial technique for economizing a movie's presentation of movement.

mechanical effect. A special effect created by an object or event mechanically on the set and in front of the camera.

A classic example of a match-on-action cut from John Ford's *Stagecoach* (1939, Walter Wanger Productions). Doc Boone enters a bar, points to a bottle of whiskey, and asks "Can I have that?" [1] Another character slides the bottle down the bar toward him. A cut to a second shot [2] shows Doc Boone catching the bottle and pouring himself a drink.

A medium close-up of Gloria Swanson from Billy Wilder's *Sunset Boulevard* (1950, Paramount Pictures).

medium close-up (MCU). A shot that shows a character from the middle of the chest to the top of the head. A medium close-up provides a view of the face that catches minor changes in expression, as well as some detail about the character's posture.

medium long shot (MLS). Also known as *plan américain* or *American shot.* A shot that shows a character from the knees up and includes most of the person's body.

A medium long shot from Fred Zinnemann's *High Noon* (1952, Stanley Kramer Productions).

medium shot (MS). A shot showing the human body, usually from the waist up.

middle-focal-length lens. Also known as *normal lens.* A lens that does not distort perspectival relations. Compare *long-focal-length lens*, *short-focal-length lens*, and *zoom lens.*

minor role. Also known as *supporting role.* A role that helps move the plot forward (and thus may be as important as a major role) but that is played by an actor who does not appear in as many scenes as the featured players do.

mise-en-scène. The composition, or staging, of all the elements within the frame, including setting, costumes and make-up, actors, lighting, and figure movement.

A medium shot from Tom Hooper's *The King's Speech* (2010, UK Film Council and See-Saw Films).

mixing. The process of combining different sound tracks onto one composite sound track that is synchronous with the picture.

montage. (a) In France, the word for editing, from the verb *monter,* meaning "to assemble or put together." (b) In the former Soviet Union in the 1920s, the various forms of editing that expressed ideas developed by theorists and filmmakers such as Sergei Eisenstein.

montage sequence. An integrated series of shots that rapidly depicts multiple related events occurring over time. Not to be confused with *montage editing*, montage sequences are used to condense time when an accumulation of actions is necessary to the narrative, but developing each individual action would consume too much of the movie's duration.

motif. A recurring visual, sound, or narrative element that imparts meaning or significance.

movie star. A phenomenon, generally associated with Hollywood, comprising the actor and the characters played by that actor, an image created by the studio to coincide with the kind of roles associated with the actor, and a reflection of the social and cultural history of the period in which that image was created.

moving frame. The result of the dynamic functions of the frame around a motion-picture image, which can contain moving action but can also move and thus change its viewpoint.

N

narration. The act of telling the story of the film. The primary source of a movie's narration is the camera, which narrates the story by showing us the events of the narrative onscreen. When the word "narration" is used to refer more narrowly to spoken narration, the reference is to commentary spoken by either an offscreen or onscreen voice. When that commentary is not spoken by one of the characters in the movie, it is *omniscient*. When spoken by a character within the movie, the commentary is *first-person narration*.

narrative. A cinematic structure in which content is selected and arranged in a cause-and-effect sequence of events occurring over time.

narrative film. Also known as *fiction film*. A movie that tells a story—with characters, places, and events—that is conceived in the mind of the film's creator. Stories in narrative films may be wholly imaginary or based on true occurrences, and they may be realistic, unrealistic, or both.

narrator. Who or what tells the story of a film. The primary narrator in cinema is the camera, which narrates the film by showing us events in the movie's narrative. When referring to the more specific action of voice narration, the narrator may be either a character in the movie (a first-person narrator) or a person who is not a character (an *omniscient* narrator).

nondiegetic element. Something that we see and hear on the screen that comes from outside the world of the movie's story (including background music, titles and credits, and voice-over narration). Compare *diegetic element.*

nonsimultaneous sound. Sound that has previously been established in the movie and replays for some narrative or expressive purpose. Nonsimultaneous sounds often occur when a character has a mental flashback to an earlier voice that recalls a conversation, or to a sound that identifies a place, event, or other significant element of the narrative. Compare *simultaneous sound.*

normal lens. See *middle-focal-length lens.*

O

oblique-angle shot. See *Dutch-angle shot.*

obstacles. Events, circumstances, and actions that impede a protagonist's pursuit of a goal. Obstacles often originate from an antagonist and are central to a narrative conflict.

offscreen sound. A form of sound, either diegetic or nondiegetic, that derives from a source we do not see on the screen. When diegetic, it consists of sound effects, music, or vocals that emanate from the world of the story. When nondiegetic, it takes the form of a musical score or a voice-over narration by someone not present onscreen. Compare *onscreen sound*.

offscreen space. Cinematic space that exists outside the frame. Compare *onscreen space*.

omniscient. Providing a third-person point of view or perspective on the movie's action or characters. Compare *restricted*.

omniscient POV. The most common point of view portrayed in movies. An omniscient POV allows the camera to travel freely within the world of the film, showing us the narrative's events from a godlike, unlimited perspective that no single character in the film could possibly have. Compare *character POV* and *group POV*.

180-degree system. Also known as the *180-degree rule*. The fundamental means by which filmmakers maintain consistent *screen direction*, orienting the viewer and ensuring a sense of the cinematic space in which the action occurs. The system depends on three factors working together in any scene: (a) the action in a scene must move along a hypothetical line that keeps the action on a single side of the camera; (b) the camera must shoot consistently on one side of that line; and (c) everyone on the production set—particularly the director, cinematographer, editor, and actors—must understand and adhere to this system.

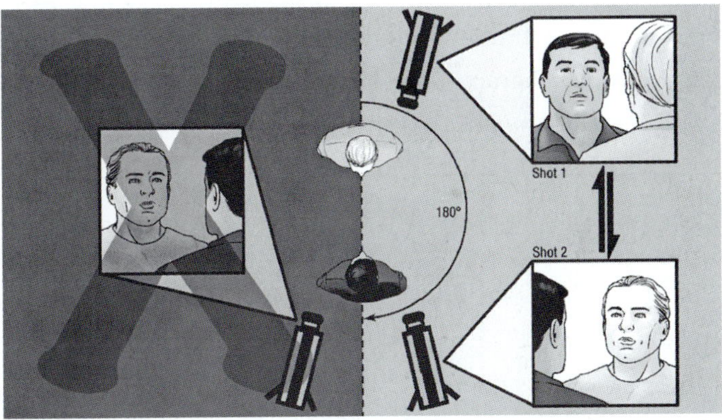

This diagram illustrates how the 180-degree system would apply to a hypothetical shoot featuring two actors facing each other. Shots 1 and 2 are taken from positions within the same 180-degree space. When viewers see the resulting shots onscreen, they can make sense of the actors' relative positions to one another. If a camera is placed in the opposite 180-degree space, the resulting shot reverses the actors' spatial orientation and thus cannot be used in conjunction with either shot 1 or shot 2 without confusing the viewer.

on location. Shooting in an actual interior or exterior location away from the studio. Compare *set*.

onscreen sound. A form of diegetic sound that emanates from a source that we both see and hear. Onscreen sound may be internal sound or external sound. Compare *offscreen sound*.

onscreen space. Cinematic space that exists inside the frame. Compare *offscreen space*.

open frame. A frame around a motion-picture image that, theoretically, characters and objects can enter and leave. Compare *closed frame*.

This shot from Robert Zemeckis's *Cast Away* (2000, Twentieth Century Fox, Dreamworks, Image Movers), set in a vast open space, is framed in a way which suggests that Tom Hanks's character has the freedom to move about as he chooses, and to leave the film frame accordingly.

outtake. Material that is not used in either the rough cut or the final cut, but is cataloged and saved.

overlap editing. An editing technique that expands viewing time and adds emphasis to an action or moment by repeating it a number of times.

overlapping sound. Sound that carries over from one shot to the next before the sound of the second shot begins.

P

pan shot. The horizontal movement of a camera mounted on the gyroscopic head of a stationary tripod.

parallel editing. Also called *crosscutting.* Cutting back and forth between two or more simultaneous actions that occur at different places. A very familiar convention in chase or rescue sequences, parallel editing often results in the convergence of the various lines of action.

plan américain. See *medium long shot.*

plane. Any of three areas—foreground, middle ground, and background—within the implied depth of the frame. See also *rule of thirds.*

plot. The specific actions and events that the filmmakers select and the order in which they arrange those events and actions to effectively convey onscreen the movie's narrative to a viewer. Compare *narrative* and *story.*

plot duration. The time that the narrative events explicitly shown onscreen are implied to have taken. Compare *screen duration* and *story duration.*

plot point. A significant event that turns the narrative in a new direction.

point of view (POV). The position from which a film presents the actions of the story; it involves not only the relation of the narrator(s) to the story but also the camera's act of seeing and hearing. The two fundamental types of cinematic point of view are *omniscient* and *restricted.*

point-of-view editing. The process of editing different shots together in such a way that the resulting sequence makes us aware of the perspective or POV of a particular character or group of characters. Most frequently, it starts with an objective shot of a character looking toward something outside of the frame, and then cuts to a shot of the object, person, or action that the character is supposed to be looking at.

1

2

3

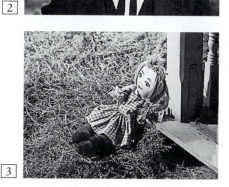

In this sequence of shots from *Night of the Hunter* (1955, Paul Gregory Productions), a young girl enters the scene and reaches out to Robert Mitchum [1], who seems to be looking down at her [2], but then we see that his gaze is fixed on the doll that the girl has dropped [3]. This POV editing sends a clear signal about Robert Mitchum's priorities and intentions.

postproduction. The third stage of the production process, consisting of editing, preparing the final print, and bringing the film to the public (marketing and distribution). Postproduction is preceded by *preproduction* and *production*.

POV. See *point of view*.

preproduction. The initial, planning-and-preparation stage of the production process. Preproduction is followed by *production* and *postproduction*.

prime lens. A lens that has a fixed focal length. The short-focal-length, middle-focal-length, and long-focal-length lenses are all prime lenses; the zoom lens, which has a variable focal length, is in its own category.

process shot. Live shooting against a background that is front- or rear-projected on a translucent screen.

producer. The person who guides the entire process of making the movie, from its initial planning to its release, and is chiefly responsible for the organizational and financial aspects of the production, from arranging the financing to deciding how the money is spent.

production. The second stage of the production process, the actual shooting. Production is preceded by *preproduction* and followed by *postproduction*.

production designer. A person who works closely with the director, art director, and director of photography in visualizing the movie that will appear on the screen. The production designer is both an artist and an executive, responsible for the overall design concept, the *look* of the movie—as well as individual sets, locations, furnishings, props, and costumes—and for supervising the heads of the many departments (art, costume design and construction, hairstyling, makeup, wardrobe, location, etc.) which create that look.

production value. The amount of human and physical resources devoted to the image, including the style of its lighting. Production value helps determine the overall style of a film.

properties. Also known as *props*. Objects used to enhance a movie's mise-en-scène by providing physical tokens of narrative information.

protagonist. The primary character whose pursuit of a goal provides the structural foundation of a movie's narrative. Compare *antagonist*.

pull focus. The technique of adjusting focus in order to maintain focus on a subject when the camera, the subject, or both are in motion through depth. Compare *rack focus*.

R

rack focus. A change of the point of focus from one subject to another within the same shot. Rack focus guides our attention to a new, clearly focused point of interest while blurring the previous subject in the shot.

real time. The actual time during which something takes place. In real time, *screen duration* and *plot duration* are exactly the same. Many directors use real time within films to create uninterrupted "reality" on the screen, but they rarely use it for entire films. Compare *cinematic time, stretch relationship,* and *summary relationship.*

reframing. A movement of the camera that adjusts or alters the composition or point of view of a shot.

reshoot. To make additional takes of a shot in order to meet the director's standards or as supplemental material for production photography.

resolution. The concluding narrative events that follow the climax and that celebrate or otherwise reflect upon the story's outcomes.

restricted. Providing a view from the perspective of a single character. For example, restricted narration reveals information to the audience only as a specific character learns of it. Compare *omniscient*.

reverse-angle shot. A shot in which the angle of shooting is opposite to that of the preceding shot.

rising action. The development of the action of the narrative toward a climax.

round character. A complex character possessing numerous subtle, repressed, or contradictory traits. Round characters often develop and change over the course of a story. Compare *flat character*.

rule of thirds. A principle of *composition* that breaks the frame into three equal vertical sections and three equal horizontal sections, resulting in a grid of nine boxes. This grid acts as a guide which filmmakers then use to balance the visual elements in the frame by threes: top, middle, bottom; left, center, right; foreground, middle ground, and background. Typically, for every visual element placed in one section, there will be a corresponding element in the opposite section to counterbalance the composition.

The grid superimposed over these two shots from the same scene in *Hidden Figures* (2016, Fox 2000 Pictures, Chernin Entertainment/Levantine Films) illustrates how the rule of thirds is used to balance compositional elements.

S

scale. The size and placement of a particular object or a part of a scene in relation to the rest—a relationship determined by the type of shot used and the placement of the camera.

scene. A complete unit of plot action incorporating one or more shots and taking place in a continuous time frame in a single location; the setting of that action.

scope. The overall range of a story.

score. Nondiegetic music that is typically composed and recorded specifically for use in a particular film, and is used to convey or enhance meaning and emotion.

screen direction. The direction of a figure's or object's movement on the screen.

screen duration. The amount of time that it has taken to present the movie's plot onscreen (i.e., the movie's running time). Compare *plot duration* and *story duration*.

screen test. A filming undertaken by an actor to audition for a particular role.

sequence. A series of edited shots characterized by inherent unity of theme and purpose.

sequence shot. See *long take*.

set. A constructed space used as the setting for a particular shot in a movie. Sets must be constructed both to look authentic and to photograph well. Compare *on location*.

setting. The time and space in which a story takes place.

setup. One camera position and everything associated with it. Whereas the shot is the basic building block of the film, the setup is the basic component of the film's production.

shooting angle. The level and height of the camera in relation to the subject being photographed. The five basic camera angles produce *eye-level shots*, *high-angle shots*, *low-angle shots*, *Dutch-angle shots*, and *aerial-view shots*.

shooting script. A guide and reference point for all members of the production unit, in which the details of each shot are listed and can thus be followed during filming.

short-focal-length lens. Also known as *wide-angle lens*. A lens that creates the illusion of depth within a frame, albeit with some distortion at the edges of the frame. Compare *long-focal-length lens*, *middle-focal-length lens*, and *zoom lens*.

shot. (a) In an edited film, an unbroken span of action captured by an uninterrupted run of the camera that lasts until it is replaced by another shot by means of a cut or other transition. (b) During the preproduction and production process, a specific arrangement of elements to be captured in a particular composition from a predetermined camera position. Compare *setup* and *take*.

A shot from Stanley Kubrick's *Dr. Strangelove* (1964, Hawk Films) that employs the short-focal-length lens.

shot / reverse shot. One of the most prevalent and familiar of all editing patterns, consisting of cuts between shots of different characters, usually in a conversation or confrontation. Sometimes the shots are framed over each character's shoulder, but other times only one character is onscreen at a time.

Two shots from Elia Kazan's *On the Waterfront* (1954, Horizon Pictures), showing a classic shot / reverse shot cut between Eva Marie Saint and Marlon Brando.

simultaneous sound. Sound that is diegetic and occurs onscreen. Compare *nonsimultaneous sound.*

slate. The board or other device that is used to identify each scene during shooting.

slow motion. Cinematographic technique that decelerates action onscreen. It is achieved by filming the action at a rate greater than the normal 24 frames per second (fps). When the shot is then played back at the standard 24 fps, cinematic time proceeds at a slower rate than the real action that took place in front of the camera.

sound effect. A sound artificially created for the sound track that has a definite function in telling the story.

soundstage. A windowless, soundproofed, professional shooting environment that is usually several stories high and can cover an acre or more of floor space.

sound track. In the sound-editing process, a single track consisting of recordings of a specific type of sound, such as a character's dialogue, sound effects, ambient sound, music, and so on. These individual sound tracks are layered during the sound-editing process, and mixed during the finishing stages of postproduction.

source light. See *key light.*

special effects (SFX, FX). Also known as *mechanical effects* and *practical effects*. Any effect generated on set that can be photographed by the camera. Special effects are used to create images that would be too dangerous, too expensive, or, in some cases, simply impossible to achieve with traditional cinematographic materials. The goal of special-effects cinematography is generally to create verisimilitude within the imaginative world of even the most fanciful movie. Compare *visual effects*.

split screen. A method, created either in the camera or during the editing process, of telling two stories at the same time by dividing the screen into different parts. Unlike parallel editing, which cuts back and forth between shots for contrast, the split screen can tell multiple stories within the same frame.

staging. See *mise-en-scène*.

stand-in. An actor who looks reasonably like a particular movie star (or at least like an actor playing a major role) in height, weight, coloring, and so on, and who substitutes for that actor during the tedious process of preparing setups or taking light readings.

Steadicam. A camera suspended from an articulated arm that is attached to a vest strapped to the cameraperson's body, permitting the operator to remain steady during "handheld" shots. The Steadicam removes jumpiness and is now often used for smooth, fast, and extended camera movement.

stock. See *film stock*.

stop-motion cinematography. A technique that allows the camera operator to stop and start the camera in order to facilitate changing the subject while the camera is not shooting. Frequently used for claymation and other forms of physical animation.

story. In a movie, all the events that we see or hear on the screen, and all the events that are implicit or that we infer to have happened but that are not explicitly presented. Compare *narrative* and *plot*.

storyboard. A breakdown that combines sketches or photographs of how each shot is to look and written descriptions of the other elements that are to go with each shot, including dialogue, sound, and music.

story duration. The amount of time that the entire narrative arc of a movie's story—whether explicitly presented onscreen or not—is implied to have taken to occur. Compare *plot duration* and *screen duration*.

stretch relationship. A time relationship in which screen duration is longer than plot duration. Compare *real time* and *summary relationship.*

stuntperson. A performer who doubles for another actor in scenes requiring special skills or involving hazardous actions, such as crashing cars, jumping from high places, swimming, or riding (or falling off) horses.

subplot. A subordinate sequence of action in a narrative, usually relevant to and enriching the plot.

summary relationship. A time relationship in which screen duration is shorter than plot duration. Compare *real time* and *stretch relationship.*

supporting role. See *minor role.*

swish pan. A type of transition between two or more shots made by moving the camera so rapidly that it blurs the moment of transition.

synopsis. A condensed description of a film's essential narrative ideas and structure. Compare *treatment.*

T

take. On a film production, one of sometimes multiple recordings of a predetermined shot. Multiple takes of a shot may be taken to remedy mistakes or to provide the editor with varied performances, blocking, or camera movements.

telephoto lens. See *long-focal-length lens.*

three-point system. Also known as *three-point lighting.* Perhaps the best-known lighting convention in feature filmmaking, a system that employs three sources of light—*key light, fill light,* and *backlight*—each aimed from a different direction and position in relation to the subject. The three-point system allows filmmakers to control the relative balance between illumination and shadow.

tilt shot. The vertical movement of a camera mounted on the gyroscopic head of a stationary tripod.

tracking shot. See *dolly shot.*

traveling shot. See *dolly shot.*

treatment. An extended prose outline of the action that relates a film's basic narrative progression. Compare *synopsis.*

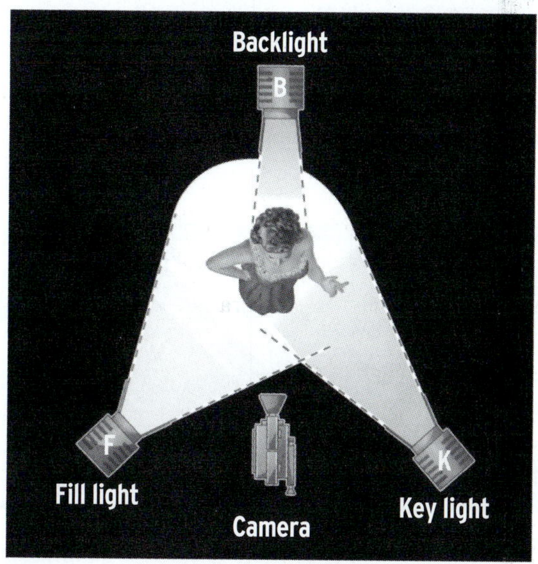

This diagram shows the setup of the classic three-point system, and this shot from Josef von Sternberg's *The Scarlet Empress* (1934, Paramount Pictures) shows how the system can be used to accentuate the glamour of stars such as Marlene Dietrich.

two-shot. A shot in which two characters appear; ordinarily a medium shot or medium long shot.

A two-shot of the Winklevoss twins from David Fincher's *The Social Network* (2010, Columbia Pictures Corporation, Relativity Media).

typecasting. The casting of actors because of their looks or "type" rather than for their acting talent or experience.

V

variable-focal-length lens. See *zoom lens.*

verisimilitude. A convincing appearance of truth; movies are verisimilar when they convince you that the things on the screen—people, places, and so on, no matter how fantastic or antirealistic—are "really there."

visual effects (VFX). Effects created and integrated using computers in postproduction. In the digital age, visual effects have largely eclipsed special effects, replacing them with digital animation that can create settings and backgrounds with more accuracy and less cost. VFX backgrounds are often employed for spectacular imaginary worlds in fantasy and science fiction films, but are also used to enhance backgrounds to allow scenes set in contemporary (and even relatively mundane) locales to be shot on a sound stage or at a more convenient location. Actors can be placed within digitally generated settings by shooting them against a uniformly colored backdrop (usually bright green, hence the term "green screen"), and then applying chroma keying, a process that digitally removes that color so that it can be replaced with computer-generated images. Compare *special effects.*

voice-over narration. Narration heard concurrently and over a scene but not synchronized to any character on the screen at the time. It can come from a third-person narrator (someone who is not a character) or a first-person narrator commenting on the action from somewhere outside of the shot's diegesis.

W

wide-angle lens. See *short-focal-length lens.*

widescreen. Any aspect ratio wider than 1.33:1.

wipe. A transitional device between shots in which shot B wipes across shot A, either vertically or horizontally, to replace it.

Z

zoom in. A shot in which the image is magnified by movement of the camera's lens only, without the camera itself moving. Compare to the *dolly in*.

zoom lens. Also known as *variable-focal-length lens*. A lens that is moved toward and away from the subject being photographed, has a continuously variable focal length, and helps to reframe a shot within the take. A zoom lens permits the camera operator during shooting to shift between wide-angle and telephoto lenses without changing the focus or aperture settings. Compare *long-focal-length lens*, *middle-focal-length lens*, and *short-focal-length lens*.